AF120210

Developing Information Literacy Skills

A GUIDE TO FINDING, EVALUATING, AND CITING SOURCES

Janine Carlock

University of Michigan Press
Ann Arbor

Copyright © by the University of Michigan 2020
All rights reserved
Published in the United States of America
The University of Michigan Press
Manufactured in the United States of America

∞ Printed on acid-free paper

ISBN-13: 978-0-472-03766-7 (paper)
ISBN-13: 978-0-472-12641-5 (ebook)

2023   2022   2021   2020   4   3   2   1

No part of this publication may be reproduced, stored in a retrieval system, or transmitted in any form or by any means, electronic, mechanical, or otherwise, without the written permission of the publisher.

Contents

Introduction   1
    How to Use This Book   4
    Defining Information Literacy   5

Lesson 1: Research as Inquiry: Defining the Scope of Your Research   8
    Choosing a Topic to Investigate   10
    Refining the Topic and Finding Relevant Research   11
    Task 1.1: Identifying Information Gaps   14
    Task 1.2: Reflecting on Narrowed Topics of Interest   14
    Lesson Connection   16

Lesson 2: Inquiry as a Path to Exploration: Identifying Key Words in the Conversation   17
    Examining Class Materials   18
    Task 2.1: Creating a Key Word List   19
    Examining Other Sources   20
    Task 2.2: Revising Your Key Word List   24
    Lesson Connection   25

Lesson 3: Scholarship as Conversation 1: Identifying Possible Directions for the Conversation   26
    Idea Maps as Tools to Identify Research Focus   27
    Task 3.1: Creating an Idea Map   28
    Task 3.2: Identifying Gaps in Idea Maps   31
    Lesson Connection   31

Lesson 4: Scholarship as Conversation 2: Understanding the Research Paradigm and Bias — 32

    Task 4.1: Reflecting on What You Have to Say — 33

    Confirmation Bias — 34

    Task 4.2: Looking at Author Word Choice for Bias — 42

    Task 4.3: Recognizing Your Own Bias — 42

    Lesson Connection — 43

Lesson 5: Using Databases to Find Sources — 44

    Academic Databases — 45

    Task 5.1: Discovering Good Databases for Particular Areas of Research — 46

    Using Databases to Conduct a Good Search — 47

    Task 5.2: Expanding Your Key Word List to Conduct an Effective Database Search — 47

    Task 5.3: Conducting a Boolean Search — 51

    Task 5.4: Comparing Characteristics of Databases — 55

    Lesson Connection — 57

Lesson 6: Reading with Purpose: The Structure of Research Article — 58

    The Structure of a Research Article — 58

    Strategies for Reading Research — 61

    Task 6.1: Reading to Find Useful Information — 63

    Bias in the Process of Reading — 64

    Lesson Connection — 66

Lesson 7: Authority Is Constructed and Contextual 1: Identifying Source Characteristics — 67

    Primary versus Secondary Sources — 67

    Currency and Place in the Information Cycle — 67

    Task 7.1: Distinguishing between Primary and Secondary Sources — 68

    Identifying Source Characteristics — 71

    Task 7.2: Investigating the Characteristics of a Source — 73

    Accessibility of Sources and Bias — 73

    Lesson Connection — 74

Lesson 8: Authority Is Constructed and Contextual 2: Examining Source Characteristics and Bias to Determine Appropriateness — 75

    Considering the *Why* to Recognize Bias — 78

    Task 8.1: Examining the Why — 79

    Determining the Appropriateness of *Where*: Assessing Authority — 79

    Task 8.2: Examining the Where — 80

    Determining the Appropriateness of *When*: Assessing Currency and Place in the Information Cycle — 80

    Task 8.3: Examining the When — 81

    Determining the Appropriateness of *Who*: Assessing Authority — 81

    Task 8.4: Examining the Who — 85

Determining the Appropriateness of *What* (Content): Assessing Relevance, Accuracy, and Comprehensiveness ... 85

Task 8.5: Examining the What ... 88

Performing a Complete Evaluation of a Source ... 89

Task 8.6: Evaluating a Source ... 94

Lesson Connection ... 94

Appendix A: Information Literacy Skills and the Research Cycle ... 95

Appendix B: Citing and Using Sources ... 97

Appendix C: Lesson Checklists ... 104

Glossary ... 109

References ... 111

Introduction

This book provides explanation of and practice with skills that enable students to find and use valid and appropriate sources for a research project, also known as **information literacy skills**. Anyone who does academic research needs these skills to accomplish their research efficiently and effectively, especially in today's world, where unauthenticated and poorly written information can be found digitally on multiple platforms. *The International Student's Guide to Writing a Research Paper* (Carlock, Eberhardt, Hurst, & Kolenich, 2017) was designed to familiarize students with the stages of writing a research paper and introducing important concepts for that task. *Developing Information Literacy Skills* focuses on providing students with the critical-thinking and problem-solving skills needed to: (1) identify the conversation that exists around a topic, (2) clarify their own perspective on that topic, and (3) efficiently and effectively read and evaluate what others have said that can inform students' perspective and research.

The focus here is not on the final product, on how to properly express ideas or format properly, but on how to ask questions to develop thinking about a problem, how to think more flexibly about an issue, and how to find relevant resources to inform thinking. After all, in the "real world," if you cannot find information one way, you have to be flexible and think of another way to get what you need. In marketing, for example, if you are not reaching your customers successfully, you have to do research to find out where the problem is; you have to know what resources you can use—*where to go and who to talk to*—to find out how to solve this problem. In engineering, if you are developing a product and it is not working, you have to think flexibly to discover where the problem actually lies and then think flexibly about who you need to consult with about the problem. Then you have to undergo a process of trial and error to refine the product. This is all part of the research process. As Einstein said, "If I had an hour to solve a problem and my life depended on the solution, I would spend the first 55 minutes determining the proper questions to ask… for once I know the proper question, I could solve the problem in less than five minutes." This book promotes development of these skills and the knowledge of how to apply them in the context of university work that can later be applied to professional contexts.

The lessons have been designed as an introduction to information literacy skills for undergraduate students. However, graduate students who are doing research but who may not have encountered the ideas introduced here may also benefit from the activities as well. The lessons have been designed to be used in a variety of contexts so that students can work through them independently or teachers can use them in a face-to-face university course, a hybrid or online course, or a series of workshops. Most lessons can done individually or in groups. Although students must work with a research topic to practice each lesson, the focus is on developing a skill, not on completing each lesson as a step toward a specific end-product like a research paper or presentation. This gives students the space to understand and reflect on how information literacy skills apply in a variety of contexts. It helps provide a better understanding how the skills they have developed in-depth can be applied to specific projects throughout their career.

The lessons can be done in order as users move through the research process or can be selected to develop specific aspects of information literacy (see Appendix A). This flexibility of use is deliberate because the research process itself requires flexibility and iterative work. If a final research project is indeed the ultimate goal, the lessons can supplement other materials, thereby serving as a **research writing companion** (see p. 4).

The choice of lesson topics and activities was guided by the literature on teaching information literacy, including the American Library Association's Framework for Information Literacy in Higher Education (see pp. 5–7).

Research as Inquiry
Scholarship as Conversation
Searching as Strategic Exploration
Information Creation as a Process
Information Has Value
Authority Is Constructed and Contextual

The frames are addressed in the book to facilitate learning and develop the skills necessary to find, read, and evaluate research. **Skills in each of these areas are valuable not only for students, but for anyone who works as part of an organization or team on the job.** The information resources may change—white papers or organizational memos and conversations will take the place of academic journals—**but the critical-thinking and problem-solving skills practiced in this book are good preparation for what students will encounter in their future workplace.**

I have been teaching information literacy for several semesters at a U.S. university, and I am excited to be able to share what I have learned. I believe that an understanding of how to find and apply relevant and valuable information to a situation is the foundation of any successful endeavor.

How to Use This Book

Lessons

Lessons 1–4 involve recognizing sources as being part of a conversation and using that conversation to develop a topic for individual research. Understanding the value of key words in research and practice recognizing and using them to develop a topic are the focus. Confirmation bias, an important concept, is introduced. These lessons could work well as a supplement to *The International Student's Guide to Writing a Research Paper* when students are developing a thesis statement (Section 2: Beginning the Process: Getting and Developing a Topic). Lesson 5 focuses specifically on databases and how to use them effectively to gain information and find support. Again, this works well in conjunction with Section 3 of *The International Student's Guide to Writing a Research Paper* (Getting Information: Working with Sources).

Lessons 6–8 offer information about sources and how to use that information to read more effectively and to evaluate sources. While this topic is covered in many writing textbooks, they do not typically offer students the opportunity to develop a critical understanding of why evaluation is so essential for their understanding of how to think critically about information.

Useful information regarding citing sources is provided in Appendix B. Checklists that will help users track their progress and reflect on their process are included in Appendix C.

A glossary of key information literacy terms is also included.

Activities

A variety of activities is provided throughout the lessons to facilitate learning and promote deeper thinking.

- Tasks offer students practice with the skills taught in each lesson and opportunities to apply them to their research topic.
- The Lesson Connection at the end of each lesson allows students to connect what they have learned in the lesson to their own life, which helps them to create an identity for themselves as researchers and to see themselves as part of a scholarly community.

Defining Information Literacy

Information literacy is the ability to find, identify, evaluate, and use information effectively, efficiently, and ethically to investigate some topic or issue.

In an era where information abounds and is accessible via multiple outlets, efficiently and successfully finding what you need can be an overwhelming task. Once you do find relevant information, recognizing which information is valid and authoritative presents a challenge. Then, once you have found useful, reliable sources, it is crucial to be able to ethically use the information found.

The Association of College and Research Libraries (ACRL), an organization dedicated to advancing learning, has created a framework for information literacy (www.ala.org.acrl/standards/ilframework) that identifies six crucial aspects of information literacy:

- Research as Inquiry
- Scholarship as Conversation
- Searching as Strategic Exploration
- Information Creation as a Process
- Information Has Value
- Authority Is Constructed and Contextual

The lessons have been designed to familiarize you with each aspect to provide a valuable understanding of information literacy that will be useful when conducting research, whether for a class paper or to find information in other contexts such as daily life or on the job.

1. **Research as Inquiry (Lessons 1–2).** Research is iterative and requires deeper and more expansive lines of thinking as you proceed: questions lead to answers, which lead to more questions. Therefore, there is a need for researchers to formulate questions, look for answers, and determine the scope and focus of the research through ongoing interaction (synthesizing information, reformulating relationships, formulating own conclusions) with the topic throughout the process of finding information.
2. **Scholarship as Conversation (Lessons 2–4).** Research contributes to an ongoing discourse with other scholars; therefore, researchers must be conscious of the fact that there will be varied perspectives and interpretations so they must try to determine how they fit into the conversation; as researchers/writers, they contribute their voices to the conversation.
3. **Searching as Strategic Exploration (Lesson 5).** Searching requires application of a variety of strategies, tools, and creative thinking to find the information that is out there and the ways use it to create one's own framework for approaching/interpreting a topic—this includes having knowledge of the technical aspects of finding information.
4. **Information Creation as a Process (all lessons).** The research process is iterative and so varies every time, meaning what is produced also will vary in terms of message and form of product; this means we must pay attention to format and have knowledge of production processes to make judgements about the usefulness of information.

5. **Information Has Value (Lessons 6–8).** Information has value in different ways—as a commodity, an educational tool, a way to influence, and/or a way to create understanding. As a result, legal issues may be involved in the production and dissemination of information. This means information users should recognize the value of proper attribution and understand how aspects of the dissemination of information, such as putting information behind a paywall or the fact that information production or gaining access to dissemination is more difficult for some than others, can influence the availability of information and the perspectives available.
6. **Authority Is Constructed and Contextual (Lessons 4, 7–8).** Information is created by authors with certain experiences, backgrounds, and attitudes, all of which shape that information. Also, authors and others (including readers/researchers) put information into a certain context. For these reasons, the authority and credibility of a source must be critically evaluated. This frame includes an understanding of the value of different contexts.

LESSON 1

Research as Inquiry: Defining the Scope of Your Research

Inquiry is the foundation of all university work. It involves conducting a structured investigation to gain a comprehensive understanding of a topic, piece of writing, speech, etc. This investigation involves **a process of asking questions to examine a topic from a variety of angles.**

There is no limit to the number of questions you can ask or to the directions that you can move while conducting inquiry. There are no right or wrong answers. Each person will have a unique path of inquiry because that path is determined by each person's knowledge and experience. For example, if one person reads something about a recent earthquake, he or she might wonder if the number of earthquakes is rising every year. Another person might wonder what process led to the earthquake. Someone else might wonder about the process of providing aid to the victims. Yet another person might look into what software programs are commonly used to accept global donations for worldwide disaster relief. Millions of questions can be asked about one event because each person's knowledge, experience, and interests are unique.

Through the process of inquiry—by asking questions—a focus is determined based on your interests, and you begin to collect information related to that focus. Then you analyze the information you have found and consult your own knowledge and experience to construct a point of view about that focus and, eventually, arrive at some conclusions. This is known as the **research cycle** (see Figure 1.1). To conduct an effective inquiry that will produce valid conclusions, you must first define the scope of your inquiry. **Scope** relates to a particular project. It means **how much or what aspect(s) of a topic you plan to tackle in your project.** The larger your topic, the more people there are who have contributed in some way to the topic. One way to think

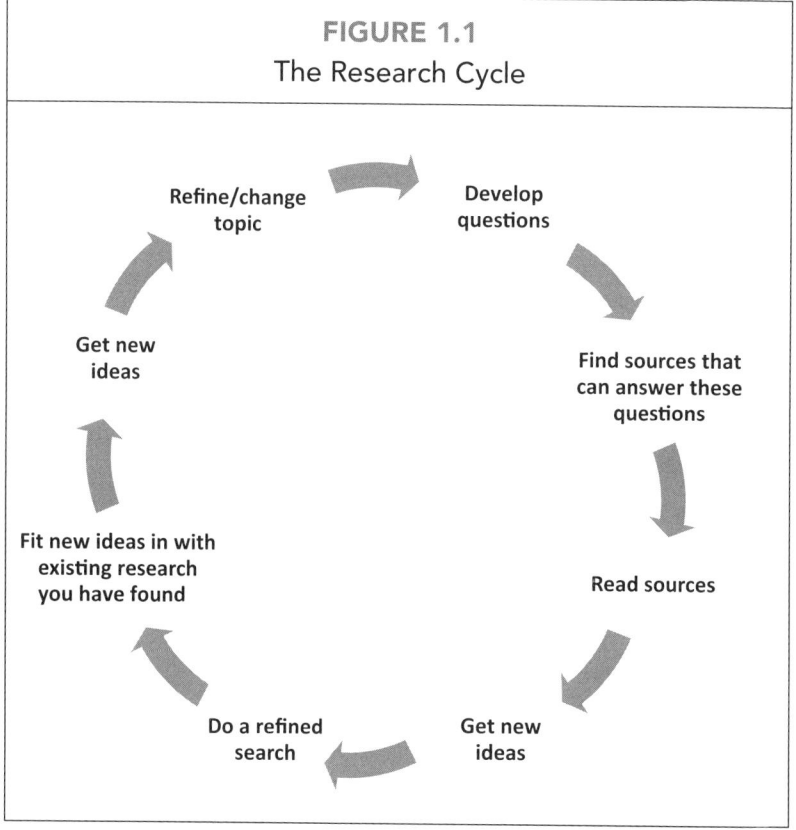

**FIGURE 1.1
The Research Cycle**

about what has been discussed about your topic is to think of it as an ongoing conversation that you want to be part of. This means that you will need to clarify what *you* want to say about the topic so that **what you have to say** will fit into the conversation.

When you select a topic, you should define it in such a way that you can contribute a unique voice to the existing conversation. Finding out what others have already said or contributed is essential, and it stimulates creativity and insight on the topic, allowing for further development. Of course, you also have to consider the **audience and purpose** of the research project as well as any **assignment requirements** as you develop your topic.

Choosing a Topic to Investigate

If you do not already have a topic to use for the tasks in the book, choose one in Table 1.1 that you would like to investigate as you complete the tasks in each lesson. The topics provided span a variety of social, economic, psychological, and political issues. They are purposefully general so that you can practice using your information literacy skills to help you find a **specific focus,** a critical skill when doing research. If you already have a topic selected that you will use for the lessons in this book, you do not need to refer to Table 1.1.

TABLE 1.1
Some Possible Research Topics

environmentally friendly cars	phone use	social media	finance
fighting cancer	urban planning	globalization	community engagement
healthy diet	making investments	music	staying healthy at college
effective learning	diversity and equity	forms of democracy (or another form of government)	immigration

Refining the Topic and Finding Relevant Research

Now that you chose a topic, consider the context of your paper. Is the topic at this stage is too specific, too broad, or at the right level to proceed to the next step of searching to find what others have said about the topic? How can you find out?

If a topic is too specific, it means that you may find that little has been written about your topic. In this case, you will need to broaden your topic so that there is a conversation to contribute to. A topic examining miles per gallon of one type of car is too specific but one looking at all hybrids is not.

More commonly, students find that they begin with a topic that is too broad. For example, all of the topics in Table 1.1 are too broad to be covered in a typical 5- to 10-page research paper (or even a book!). If a topic is too broad, then you will find a confusingly large number of related resources and will have to consider the voices of too many people as you do your research. In that case, it will be difficult to focus in on a topic to explore it in appropriate depth. You must narrow your topic to a scope that is appropriate for the context you are writing in. The topic of "why animals become extinct" is too broad for a paper this length, but the topic "the impact of game hunting in Africa" is not.

> ## Research Tip
>
> Perform a search in an academic database such as Google Scholar or EBSCO (see Lesson 5) to find academic sources. If you find more than several hundred, then your topic is likely too broad. If you only find a few, it is most likely too narrow. Note that "appropriate scope" depends on the assignment requirements. Be sure to consult with your instructor to be sure that your topic is indeed appropriate in scope.

Naming the Topic: Identifying Information Gaps

One important information literacy step to ensure your topic has appropriate scope is to identify **information gaps,** or holes in what you know about a topic. Ask yourself:

- What do I know?
- What do I not know?
- What would I like to know?

One way to identify information gaps is to take time to develop several questions about the research. These questions will give you critical information to determine what you would like to explore about the topic **before you start searching** for sources to see what others have already said about it. Figure 1.2 provides sample questions on the topic recycling. Task 1.1 asks you to answer the same questions for your own topic. In Task 1.2, you will answer questions to help narrow your focus.

FIGURE 1.2
Identifying Information Gaps for the Topic Recycling

1. Where are the information gaps for your topic? Write these gaps in the form of who, what, when, where, why, and how questions.
   a. How do different countries approach recycling?
   b. What is the process used to recycle glass or paper or …?
   c. How does the process for recycling differ for different materials?
   d. What are sample policies used at the local, state, and federal levels in the U.S.?
   e. What policies do governments use to encourage recycling?
   f. Why do some people choose to recycle while others do not?
   g. How much garbage in the U.S. (or a more specific place) is going into landfills?
   h. What harm does all this garbage cause?
   i. What are the benefits of recycling?

2. What do you know about your topic? What else do you think you need to know that you do not know about your topic? What do you know about what others have said about your topic? Include researcher names if possible. Use the questions in #1 to help you think about this.
   a. I know that recycling rules in the U.S. are determined by the local government.
   b. The rules vary as to what is required to be recycled.
   c. I am not aware of any punishment for not recycling.
   d. I do not know what the process is once the garbage collectors pick up the recycling or how the process varies in different locations.
   e. I do not know where all the garbage is taken or what environmental or health impacts it is having.
   f. I do know that certain materials can have a harmful impact environmentally by polluting the water systems and making land uninhabitable.
   g. I do know that people often resist recycling because it is inconvenient, but I don't know by what methods they can be motivated to practice recycling in daily life.
   h. I do not know the costs of recycling for companies/governments.
   i. I do not know what can be recycled.
   j. I do not know what products can be made from recycled materials.

Task 1.1

Identifying Information Gaps

1. What is your topic?

2. Where are the information gaps for your topic? Write these gaps in the form of who, what, when, where, why, and how questions.

3. What do you know about your topic? What else do you think you need to know that you do not know about your topic? What do you know about what others have said about your topic? Include researcher names if possible. Use the questions provided in #1 of Figure 1.2 to help you think about this.

Task 1.2

Reflecting on Narrowed Topics of Interest

Examine the information gaps that you identified in Task 1.1. Identify two or three possible narrowed topics of interest that you can see might be interesting. Explain why you are interested in each one to help you further narrow your topic as you proceed. An example has been provided using the recycling topic.

> Model reflection for topic recycling
>
> My information gaps identified in Task 1.1 seem to have three main themes: types of recycling, policies, and environmental impacts. Three possible narrowed topics and the reasons I would choose them:

Possible Topic 1: plastic recycling

This a specific type of recycling I am interested in with all the waste that is being created from used water bottles, frozen food packaging, etc. I know there are different grades of plastic and some are recyclable while others are not. Perhaps I could look at the cost of different types of plastic and how this influences what companies choose to use. Perhaps I will look at efforts in different places to persuade people to recycle their plastic more to see what works and what doesn't.

Possible Topic 2: local government policy-making on recycling

I am interested in improvement of my own local living situation, so I would like to examine policies for Pittsburgh, where I live, to determine the most effective practices and perhaps get involved in the policy-making process. If I can't find enough information on Pittsburgh (the topic is too narrow), I will broaden it to Western Pennsylvania.

Possible Topic 3: the most sustainable forms of recycling

I am interested in the environment and sustainability and I do not know anything about the recycling process. I would like to know more about it in terms of sustainability. I realize this is still a fairly broad topic, and as I learn more I will see how I can further narrow it—right now because I know so little, I can't really be more specific.

What are three possible narrowed topics for your work? Why might each work?

Lesson Connection

Review the information and tasks in this lesson. Write a paragraph that includes:

- *what* you learned in this particular lesson.
- *how* it is significant for you.
- *why* it is important for you to know.

Be sure to consider: *Which* information/activities were most valuable for you and *why*? How might you use this information in the future?

LESSON 2

Inquiry as a Path to Exploration: Identifying Key Words in the Conversation

When you are working on a research project and hoping to become part of the discussion, you must decide what you want to say about the topic. To do that, first you must have a clear understanding of the topic. **Key words** are concepts that are important to understanding your topic. You cannot develop your ideas, find others who are talking about your topic, or understand what others are saying about it without knowing the key words others are using in the conversation. But how do we find key words or even identify them?

Once you have a somewhat narrowed topic to explore, you already have some key words to work with: the words you use to express your topic. For example, for the topic of recycling, we can identify *plastic, policy,* and *sustainability* as possible key words. One way to help you follow the conversation is to keep a running list of key words. This will help you continue to refine your topic and to develop the ideas that can help you frame your own perspective. Later, you will also see how effective key words enable you to conduct a good search for other sources related to your topic (see Lesson 5).

To begin your list, look closely at course materials and other relevant sources. What words appear over and over?

Examining Class Materials

Your course materials—especially the course description, the syllabus, and the assignment—offer a place to start when it comes to key words. For example: Imagine that your research paper on recycling is a part of a course called "Sustainable World" and that the course description looks like this:

> Course Overview: <u>Sustainable</u> World and its companion class, Sustainable Cities, will introduce you to the field of sustainability and explore the fundamental question of how human and natural <u>systems interact</u>. Sustainable World focuses more on how the <u>environment</u> functions, but also addresses how <u>humans interact with the environment</u>: how we shape the environment and how it shapes us. This class will also focus on a general approach to solving sustainability problems that come from an emerging field known as <u>Sustainability Science</u>. Using real-world issues and problems such as <u>biodiversity loss</u>, <u>agriculture</u>, and the <u>Phoenix water system</u>, you will learn about the fundamental <u>Earth systems</u> on which we depend and how people interact with these systems.

Many important concepts for the course are underlined here for you, including *sustainable, interact, environment, biodiversity*. These provide clues as to what ideas people involved in the conversation about this topic (those in the field, experts, policymakers, etc.) are likely discussing. To join this conversation, you must be familiar with key words like these.

Task 2.1

Creating a Key Word List

1. If you have chosen a topic related to one of your courses, write key words and phrases from your course description, syllabus, and assignment to get an idea of what concepts are part of the conversation in this area. If you are using a topic provided in Lesson 1, brainstorm some possible key words for that topic based on your own knowledge.

Examining Other Sources

Go to Google or other search engines, as well as databases or other places you use to find sources for your research. Then type in some of the key words on your list. Once you get some search results, pay attention to:

- The words in the **titles** of the papers. Figure 2.1 shows the list of **titles** returned from a search in Google Scholar using the key words *sustainable, interact, environment,* or *biodiversity*. Possible key words from the list are: *ecological engineering, agricultural, ecosystem, human well-being, designing, interaction, population, diets, food production, protection, nutrition,* and *health*.

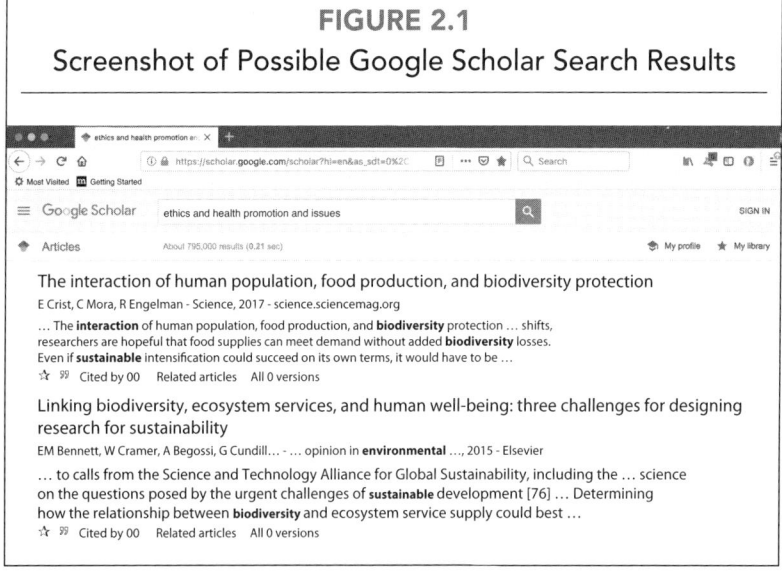

FIGURE 2.1
Screenshot of Possible Google Scholar Search Results

- The words used in the **abstracts** of the paper (found at the beginning of articles, see p. 58) that seem related to your topic. Sometimes you will find a list of key words after the abstract as well. Figure 2.2 is the **abstract** for the second article listed in Figure 2.1.
- Possible key words from the sample abstract are: *sustainable resource use, decision-making, natural resources, improve human well-being, co-produced, social-ecological systems, benefits, best practices, governance, ecosystem management, ecoSERVICES, DIVERSITAS, Future Earth, foster global coordination,* or *multidisciplinary.* Note that you may want to use an entire phrase as well as the individual words within the phrase.

FIGURE 2.2

Abstract for *"Linking Biodiversity, Ecosystem Services, and Human Well-Being: Three Challenges for Designing Research for Sustainability"* (article)

Ecosystem services have become a mainstream concept for the expression of values assigned by people to various functions of ecosystems. . . . see a need to broaden the scope of research to answer three key questions that we believe will improve incorporation of ecosystem service research into decision-making for the sustainable use of natural resources to improve human well-being: (i) how are ecosystem services co-produced by social–ecological systems, (ii) who benefits from the provision of ecosystem services, and (iii) what are the best practices for the governance of ecosystem services? Here, we present . . . a globally coordinated research programme aimed towards improving sustainable ecosystem management. These questions will frame the activities of ecoSERVICES, formerly a DIVERSITAS project and now a project of Future Earth, in its role as a platform to foster global coordination of multidisciplinary sustainability science through the lens of ecosystem services.

- The words included in some of the references in the **references section** (see Table 6.1) of related papers. A sample of a search of a reference list is shown in Figure 2.3. Possible key words from the reference list are: *controversies, service, tradeoffs, diverse landscapes, current status, prospects, marine, coastal, stakeholder, priority, biodiversity loss,* or *impact.*
- The content of any articles that look interesting.

FIGURE 2.3

Partial References List from *"Linking Biodiversity, Ecosystem Services, and Human Well-Being: Three Challenges for Designing Research for Sustainability"* (article)

---

9. Barnaud C, Antona M: **Deconstructing ecosystem services: uncertainties and controversies around a socially constructed concept.** *Geoforum* 2014, **56**:113-123.

10. Raudsepp-Hearne C, Peterson GD, Bennett EM: **Ecosystem service bundles for analyzing tradeoffs in diverse landscapes.** *Proc Natl Acad Sci USA* 2010, **107**:5242-5247.

11. Carpenter SR, Mooney HA, Agard J, Capistrano D, DeFries R, Dı́az S, Dietz T, Duraiappah AK, Oteng-Yeboah A, Pereira HM et al.: **Science for managing ecosystem services: beyond the Millennium Ecosystem Assessment.** *Proc Natl Acad Sci USA* 2009, **106**:1305-1312.

13. Abson DJ, Von Wehrden H, Baumgartner S, Fischer J, Hanspach J, Hardtle W, Heinrichs H, Klein AM, Lang DJ, Martens P et al.: **Ecosystem services as a boundary object for sustainability.** *Ecol Econ* 2014, **103**:29-37.

25. Cardinale BJ, Duffy JE, Gonzalez A, Hooper DU, Perrings C, Venail P, Narwani A, Mace GM, Tilman D, Wardle DA et al.: **Biodiversity loss and its impact on humanity.** *Nature* 2012, **486**:59-67.

Now, you should have a substantial list of key words. Table 2.1 provides an example of how you might organize a revised list. This list provides a broader picture of the important issues related to the topic *sustainable world*.

TABLE 2.1
Revised Key Word List

	Key Words from Other Sources		
Key Words from Class Materials	Related Titles from Google Search	Sample Article Abstract	Sample Article Reference List
sustainable	*ecological engineering*	*sustainable resource use*	*controversies*
interact	*agricultural*	*decision-making*	*service*
environment	*ecosystem*	*natural resources*	*tradeoffs*
biodiversity	*human well-being*	*improve human well-being*	*diverse landscapes*
	designing	*co-produced*	*current status*
	interaction	*social-ecological systems*	*prospects*
	population	*benefits*	*marine*
	diets	*best practices*	*coastal*
	food production	*governance*	*stakeholder*
	protection	*ecosystem management*	*priority*
	nutrition	*ecoSERVICES*	*biodiversity loss*
	health	*DIVERSITAS*	*impact*
		Future Earth	
		foster global coordination	
		multidisciplinary	

It is now time to start looking for a possible focus to help you further clarify your topic and the perspective—**the specific conversation** you wish your research to become part of. Looking at the key words from Table 2.1, we can imagine that some possible areas to focus on might be:

- sustainability and human well-being
- designing sustainable ecosystem management systems
- biodiversity loss as a result of unsustainable practices
- how to foster global coordination in sustainability efforts
- an examination of existing global sustainability efforts, such as *ecoSERVICES* and *DIVERSITAS* (now project Future Earth)
- sustainable agriculture and human health

Task 2.2

Revising Your Key Word List

1. Conduct a search in Google Scholar using two or three key words for your topic. Consider the search results, particularly any titles, abstracts, or reference lists of articles or books that fit your topic idea so far. What key words would you add to your list? Create a revised list like that in Table 2.1.

2. Using the list you created for #1, make a list of possible areas to focus based on your new list. What conversations would you like to explore more? Make a list of at least four possible specific conversations that you might want to explore.

RESEARCH TIP

You may want to save the articles or sources that have come up during this search as possible references for your research paper in a Word or Google document. Be sure to list important publication information so you can find them again and so you have them for your bibliography.

Lesson Connection

Review the information and tasks in this lesson. Write a paragraph that includes:

- *what* you learned in this particular lesson.
- *how* it is significant for you.
- *why* it is important for you to know.

Be sure to consider: *Which* information/activities were most valuable for you and *why*? How might you use this information in the future?

LESSON 3

Scholarship as Conversation 1: Identifying Possible Directions for the Conversation

Finding the key words on your topic (Lesson 2) is crucial for determining the scope of your research. Lesson 3 addresses developing an understanding of the key words on your topic and their relationships to one another. This allows you to move forward in your exploration of a topic because it helps you to **identify possible conversations** around the topic, which helps in the search for what other people have said about it. This is important because identifying others' perspectives will help you clarify your perspective for your project. The information from experts will act as support for your research so that what you say becomes part of the larger conversation.

Idea Maps as Tools to Identify Research Focus

One way to identify how broad or narrow key words/ideas are in relation to one another and what relationships may exist among them is to use **idea maps**. Examples of relationships are *process, comparing/contrasting,* or *causes/effect*. By identifying relationships visually, you will have a better idea of which area you might want to focus on as you continue your research. Figure 3.1 shows an idea map for the Sustainable World conversation started in Lesson 2. It uses ideas from Table 2.1 and the list on page 24.

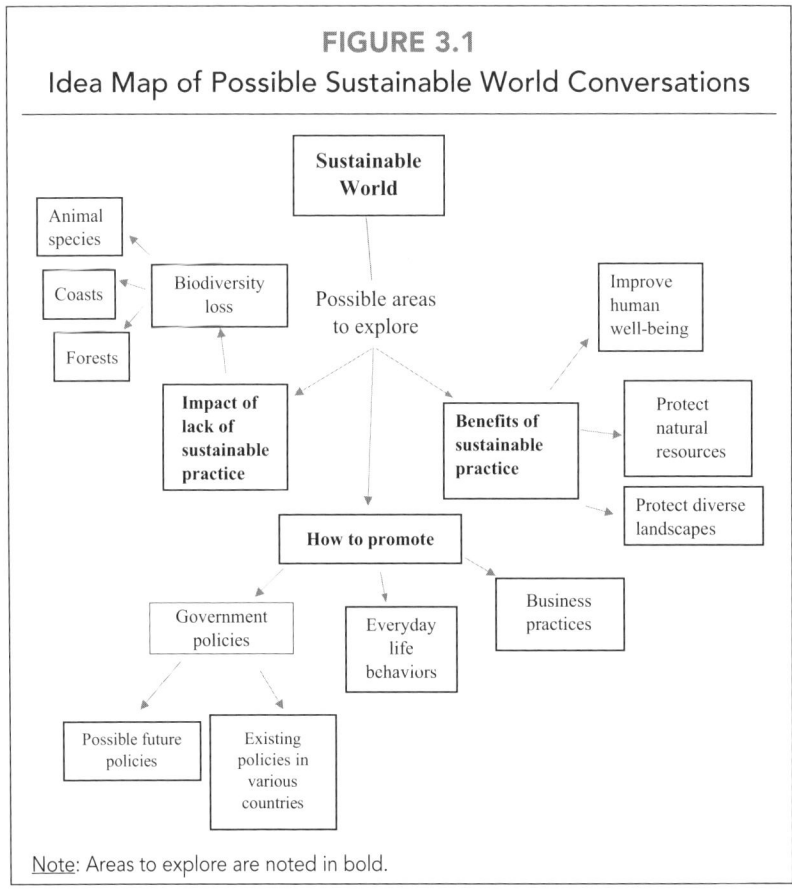

Task 3.1

Creating an Idea Map

1. On a separate sheet of paper, draw an idea map that shows the key words that you feel you would like to focus on and their relationships to one another.

What to Do with Idea Maps

A visual representation can be a guide to help you notice relationships or gaps. It can help you choose which area of the map you would like to focus on—where will you enter the conversation?

Make a list of questions to help you focus. Gaps in the idea map or areas of imbalance (too much in some areas and not enough in others) also help with focus and provide a direction for future research. Gaps and imbalances may be investigated through questions:

- I need to decide which area of the map I want to focus on: impacts? benefits? how to promote? something else? (In which direction do I want to go?)
- Am I interested in business practices? government policies? (In which direction do I want to go with "how to promote"?)
- Do I want to focus on one impact and look in depth at the process by which it occurs? Or do I want to discuss more than one? (Gap: What are impacts other than "biodiversity loss"?)
- Where do costs fit in? (Gap: costs)
- Do I want to look at how costs impact whether policies are made? how costs determine whether businesses implement sustainable practices? (Gap: What is the relationship between costs and policies or costs and implementation?)

- Do I want to look at sustainable practices and how they vary in cost? (Gap?)
- What new key words come to mind after thinking about this and seeing connections?
- Is there something else that I have thought of to add to the map?

Choose one question or a group of questions to help you refine an area of research.

Using your notes and original idea map, identify where there may be gaps in the conversation. This is especially important if your assignment asks you to pursue a unique line of investigation. You may want to look at the relationships you have found to see where you can add more boxes for balance in an area that is imbalanced. The added boxes are areas that require more research.

RESEARCH TIP

Keep all drafts of your idea maps so that you have a record of your ideas. You can return to them periodically as your research evolves.

Figure 3.2 is a revised idea map for the Sustainable World project with topics added based on the questions listed and gaps or imbalances in the original idea map. Ideas added based on analysis of Figure 3.1 are shown in italics.

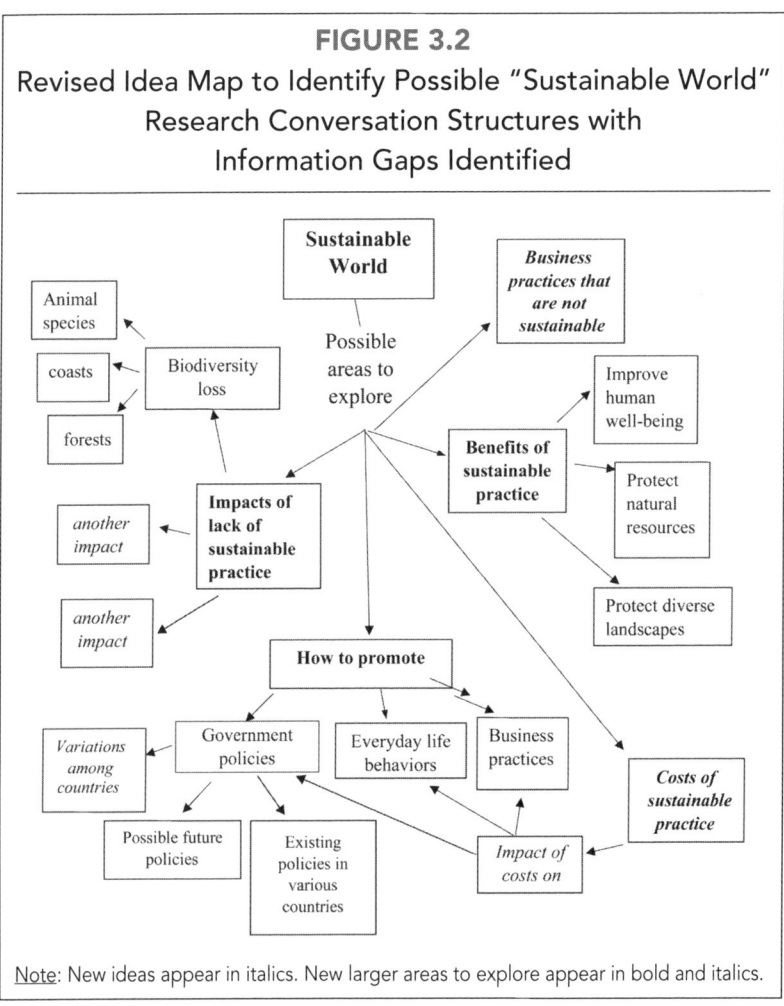

FIGURE 3.2
Revised Idea Map to Identify Possible "Sustainable World" Research Conversation Structures with Information Gaps Identified

Note: New ideas appear in italics. New larger areas to explore appear in bold and italics.

Task 3.2

Identifying Gaps in Idea Maps

1. Look at what you created in Task 3.1. Write a few questions about ideas you get from the map regarding what you should pursue in your research. Then note where you see information gaps. What is missing?

2. Where is there a possible lack of balance? What could you add? Add to your idea map based on your notes.

Lesson Connection

Review the information and tasks in this lesson. Write a paragraph that includes:

- *what* you learned in this particular lesson.
- *how* it is significant for you.
- *why* it is important for you to know.

Be sure to consider: *Which* information/activities were most valuable for you and *why*? How might you use this information in the future?

LESSON 4

Scholarship as Conversation 2: Understanding the Research Paradigm and Bias

People have their own individual motivations for doing research based on their personal experiences and interests and on how they interpret the world. This means that each person has a unique way of (1) approaching their own research on a topic and (2) interpreting others' research. As a result, if 10 people looked at the very same sources on a topic, what they would see as significant would be unique to each person's own perspective and experience. If we all choose what is important based on our own background knowledge and way of thinking about the world, what does this mean? It means that **research is done by people so it is inherently biased.**

Like anyone else, researchers are influenced subconsciously by their own motivations and by how they define reality. As a result, how their research is framed and how their results are interpreted are subject to bias.

What does this mean for your research process? To help you identify your biases as a researcher, Task 4.1 asks you to consider your relationship to your topic before going further.

As you refine your topic, refer to the questions in Task 4.1 to consider how bias may be influencing or may have influenced your choices.

Task 4.1

Reflecting on What You Have to Say

1. What is your topic at this point?

2. Which aspects do you plan to investigate?

3. What will they add to the conversation?

4. What interests you about each of these aspects?

5. What do you want your audience to learn from your paper? What are your goals? Do you hope to inform some action or influence decision- or policymaking in some way? If so, how?

6. What results do you think you will find?

7. What sources/types of sources do you think you will use as you conduct your research? Why?

Write a paragraph of 150–200 words that includes the answers to these questions. This will create a draft of what you may end up using in a research proposal for a high-stakes research project and provide you with a focus to stay on track as you continue with the research process. As you continue to identify gaps, new relationships, and biases, the description will evolve.

Confirmation Bias

Bias is something that often enters the research process without the researcher recognizing it. Several different types of bias exist. In fact, the Cognitive Bias Codex on Wikipedia shows a breakdown of almost 200 types of bias. The questions in Task 4.1 are meant to help you examine your own views/position on the topic and to analyze your motives as a way to make these biases more transparent.

It is very important for you to be aware of and reflect continuously on your research and selection process because your own **confirmation bias** can influence the choices you make in selecting sources and **cherry picking** (see p. 64) can influence the choices you make in selecting information to use from sources.

Confirmation bias (also known as *the filter bubble*) causes you to:

1. use search terms that unconsciously reflect your position/perspective.
2. unconsciously select information or resources that support your point of view.
3. not select or unconsciously ignore information or resources that do not support your point of view.

Avoiding Confirmation Bias

Strategy 1—Choose key words in your searches that do NOT cause the database to limit the sources found to those that support your point of view.

Let's say that you are writing a paper on gun control. You believe that citizens owning guns can only lead to more gun violence, and so you use key words such as *gun control*, *violence*, or *death* in your search. These key words are inherently expressing your point of view that private gun ownership leads to negative outcomes, which is limiting what your results are and, therefore, what you see/read.

The result is that you do not explore the topic comprehensively and so cannot conduct a thorough and accurate analysis.

To use Strategy 1, add other key words to avoid bias and get alternate points of view. For example, adding the word *laws* is a more neutral term that people on either side of the issue might use in their research. Also, the words *impact* or *influence* broaden perspectives from specific negative impacts with words like *violence* and *death*.

Strategy 2—Choose sources that reflect a variety of viewpoints, not just ones that support your point of view, so that you can provide a more comprehensive discussion. How do you know what viewpoint is being represented? Look at language choices made by the author in the title and paper.

Let's say that you obtain a list of articles from a general search using a fairly neutral phrase: *gun control statistics*. In selecting scholarly articles, you see these titles:

a. "The Case for Moderate Gun Control"
b. "Easiness of Legal Access to Concealed Firearm Permits and Homicide Rates in the United States"
c. "Against Moderate Gun Control"
d. "Gun Control and the Regulation of Fundamental Rights"
e. "The Effectiveness of Gun Control Laws"
f. "Does the Declining Lethality of Gunhsot Injuries Mask a Rising Epidemic of Gun Violence in the United States?"
g. "When Gun Control Costs Lives"

You choose a, b, f, and g because they look like good sources to support your position that we need more gun control.

The result is that you do not explore the topic comprehensively and so cannot conduct a thorough and accurate analysis.

To use Strategy 2, look carefully at (1) the words and relationships in the title of each article and (2) your choices to be sure you are creating a comprehensive picture of the issue.

Table 4.1 shows an example of a possible bias analysis using Strategy 2.

TABLE 4.1
Sample Bias Analysis for Titles Related to Topic of Gun Control

Article Title	Possible Bias	Words That Indicate Author Bias and Explanation of Bias
a. "The Case for Moderate Gun Control"	supporting gun control	*The case for* means the author is supporting gun control. *moderate* means that the author may not support all gun control but certain types of laws.
b. "Easiness of Legal Access to Concealed Firearm Permits and Homicide Rates in the United States"	supporting gun control	*easiness of legal access*–the choice of the word *easiness* implies an attitude that the laws are not tough enough. *and homicide rates*–puts *legal access* and *homicide rates* in comparison to indicate that easiness of legal access might be related to homicide rates in a negative way.
c. "Against Moderate Gun Control"	supporting or against?	*against* implies the author is against gun control. but *against moderate gun control* may imply that the author is supporting stricter laws.
d. "Gun Control and the Regulation of Fundamental Rights"	against	This title puts *gun control* and *regulation of fundamental rights* in opposition to one another. *Rights* are something that Americans believe we all have and the government should not deny, so this seems to be against gun control.
e. "The Effectiveness of Gun Control Laws"	neutral?	*effectiveness* could be showing a positive or negative relationship.
f. "Does the Declining Lethality of Gunshot Injuries Mask a Rising Epidemic of Gun Violence in the United States?"	supporting	*mask*–indicates that the author is questioning the way statistics are being interpreted, that fewer deaths does not mean there is less gun violence, so this source seems to be supporting gun control.
g. "When Gun Control Costs Lives"	against	*gun control costs lives* is creating a cause-effect relationship where gun control is causing people to die–focusing on this negative relationship means the author must be against some forms of gun control.

Note that the gun control issue is fairly straightforward as people generally choose a side: they are either for or against. With some issues, however, the biases are not as clear. Be sure to look at the titles in your search carefully.

Bias Analysis: Looking at Word Choice in the Text

Imagine you find a title that you think might work. Once you do that, it's time to look at word choice in the title and the text.

Reporting Verbs

One way to identify author bias is to examine how the author introduces another person's research into the article. To introduce an outside source, an author will often use the outside source author's name and possibly their qualifications and a reporting verb.

A **reporting verb** reveals the attitude of the author toward the outside source being cited, thus revealing perspective on a topic. Table 4.2 is a good reference list for identifying when reporting verbs are revealing the bias of the author. Note, however, that choice of reporting verb can still show bias even when a seemingly neutral reporting verb is used because the author's understanding of the source is shaped by personal beliefs.

TABLE 4.2
A List of Common Reporting Verbs and Their Purpose

Summarizing Reporting Verbs (Neutral)	
addresses	indicates
analyzes	interprets
believes	investigates
claims	expresses concern about
comments on	lists
compares	notes
contrasts	observes
concludes	offers
considers…in detail	points out
delineates	predicts
demonstrates	presents
describes	proposes
determines	provides evidence for
develops	recognizes
distinguishes	remarks
examines	reports
explains	shows
explores	states
finds	studies
focuses on	summarizes
gives	thinks
highlights	
identifies	

TABLE 4.2

A List of Common Reporting Verbs and Their Purpose (continued)

Putting the Original Source Author in Conversation with Other Outside Source Authors (Neutral)	Showing the Original Source Author's Individual Position (Neutral)	Showing the Research Writer's Opinion of What the Original Source Author Has Done (or Not Done) (Showing Bias)
affirms	advises	alleges
agrees	advocates	confirms
argues	asserts	doesn't mention
challenges	calls for	excludes
concurs	cautions	fails to take into account
contends	demands	
contradicts	emphasizes	favors
counters	insists	glosses over
criticizes	maintains	ignores
dismisses	opposes	implies
disputes	questions	neglects
elaborates	stresses	omits
extends	suggests	proves
objects to	urges	reveals
refutes	warns	speculates
rejects		
responds to		
takes issue with		

"Hidden" Bias Words

Other words to be aware of are words that may not signal bias in an obvious way. One example is **comparatives**. These are *–er or -est words* such as *better than* or *the greatest*. These words can be used to encourage the reader to believe the content of an article. For example, if the author is writing about a policy that he or she feels is threatening to the United States and begins with *There is no doubt that the United States is the greatest nation in the world* and the reader also believes that, it establishes a trust that the author shares similar beliefs. The result of this is that then the reader is likely to trust that what the author says elsewhere in the article.

Another example is words like *should, could,* or *might*. Taken out of context, it seems clear that these are words that indicate opinion, but in an article, sometimes they are hard to notice. They are used to **hedge**, meaning the author cannot claim with absolute certainty that something is definitely true. However, just by making the association between two items, the author is connecting them in the readers mind. Sometimes as readers, we do not remember the strength of the claim and make it stronger than it actually is.

On the other hand, sometimes the author will use a simple present tense verb to state that something is a fact. Is it really? When the author draws conclusions about situations or creates a relationship between two items by using the simple present and including the word *is,* don't be misled! You need to recognize when the author is taking advantage of this to present opinion as fact. Be sure to check for evidence for any claims the author makes. An example is *Ozone depletion will continue unless we do something to stop it.* In fact, ozone depletion also occurs due to natural causes. Humans can take some action to decrease the rate of depletion, but it will continue regardless.

In today's world of unvetted information (information not checked for truth) and fewer gatekeepers, once an idea is published, it can be republished in several sources almost immediately without anyone checking to see if it is true. In the process, the language in which it is reported changes, making it is difficult to distinguish what is fact and what is interpretation. It is therefore up to the reader and researcher to do the work to inform themselves. Lessons 7 and 8 discuss more ways of evaluating sources that you have found.

Examples of Bias in Word Choice

One example of a bias analysis taken from stories in news sources online can be found at https://reason.com/2019/10/25/environmentalists-torment-rather-than-convince-california/.

> **Why Do Environmentalists Seem Determined To Torment, Rather Than Convince?**
>
> Steven Greenhut
>
> From plastic bag bans to plastic straw bans to bans on shampoo bottles in hotels, California is adopting supposedly environmental policies that won't save the environment but will piss off residents.

Notice:

- *torment* rather than *convince*. This indicates an attitude that environmentalists are going about achieving their ends the wrong way.
- *supposedly*. This indicates an attitude of disbelief that the policies will actually protect the environment in any substantial way.
- *piss off residents*. This is the opinion of the author, or emotional language. Does he provide evidence to support this opinion?
- Possible audience. People who are not environmentalists and feel the laws to protect the environment are too strict.

Task 4.2

Looking at Author Word Choice for Bias

1. Identify the reporting verbs the author uses in the text. Examine the article for nouns, verbs, adjectives, or adverbs that indicate the opinion of the author (including comparatives and *should/could/might*).

2. What have you discovered about possible biases of the author?

3. How does this opinion fit into the context of other articles?

4. Can this article still be used in your paper despite its bias? Why or why not? (Remember, there are levels of bias. Bias is inherent in all of the author's choices and so is always present in some form or another.)

Task 4.3

Recognizing Your Own Bias

1. Use Strategy 1. Look at your list of key words. Add two or three neutral words that will help you to avoid bias in a search for resources.

2. Use Strategy 2. Do your own search and find a list of articles to choose from. Analyze at least five of the titles you find in the same way that were done in Table 4.1 for the topic of gun control.

Summary of Bias Analysis

Do your article choices show bias? In what way(s) do your sources present a similar view of the topic? In what way(s) do your sources cover the topic differently?

Looking at the research plan that you created at the beginning of the lesson and any evidence of your own bias in selecting articles, how have your ideas about your research topic changed? What further refining of your topic might be possible to make your own biases clear?

Lesson Connection

Review the information and tasks in this lesson. Write a paragraph that includes:

- *what* you learned in this particular lesson.
- *how* it is significant for you.
- *why* it is important for you to know.

Be sure to consider: *Which* information/activities were most valuable for you and *why*? How might you use this information in the future?

LESSON 5

Using Databases to Find Sources

When doing research, you must sort through a multitude of sources in a variety of formats to find the best information to flesh out your topic and see how to fit what you have to say into the existing conversation. Databases are a great place to start.

A database (typically digital) stores and organizes information so that it can easily be retrieved. Common online databases you likely already know that you can access for free are Wikipedia or IMDb. These are useful for finding information in everyday life, but not for academic work. Google Scholar is an online database that allows you to search for academic sources and is free.

You have no doubt used the search engine Google many times to find information on the internet. However, much of the information on the internet has not been evaluated by anyone to ensure it is valid and reliable (see Lesson 7). While Google may be useful when seeking sources for an academic paper, remember that Google does use an algorithm when searching, which creates a search bias. This means that if a source does not rate high for Google, even if it might be useful for you, it may be far down the list and you may not even see it listed. (For more information on how Google rates sites, see https://blog.hubspot.com/marketing/google-ranking-algorithm-infographic.) Therefore, academic databases are the preferred area to search for information and resources for an academic paper. See Appendix B for things to consider once you start citing and using sources as you write your paper.

Academic Databases

Academic databases have countless sources that can support an academic paper. They include sources in various formats and related to many topics. Unlike Wikipedia or Google, however, most academic databases do not offer free access (Google Scholar is one of the few). Therefore, a key resource that you can take advantage of as a university student is your university library because it pays fees so you have free access to many databases.

Some academic databases contain sources related to one field, such as health information or literature, which can sometimes help you in your search by already narrowing it to a certain area. Others are more general databases that contain sources valuable for a variety of academic fields.

In either case, library databases provide you with a structured way to access thousands of academic journals, trade publications, magazines, news sources, and books that you otherwise would have to buy or pay to read.

Some common databases to use to get background information are:

- Google Scholar
- Credo Reference
- CQ Researcher

Some commonly used databases for research that are not field-specific are:

- Academic Search
- ProQuest
- JStor
- ERIC/EBSCO

Each university library decides which databases to subscribe to depending on its student population. If your university has a medical school, for example, the library may have more medical and health-related databases. Before you begin your research, you should visit your library's website and complete any tutorials on using databases. You should also talk with your professors and university librarians to find out which databases might be the most useful to use for a search in your discipline or for your particular topic.

Task 5.1

Discovering Good Databases for Particular Areas of Research

1. Talk with a librarian at your university. Which databases are recommended for doing research in different subject areas? Which areas are recommended for your discipline?

2. Look at the information you can find in Credo Reference and CQ Researcher on recycling, sustainability, gun control, or your own topic. Compare this information with the information and types of sources that are listed when you search in Academic Search Premier/Elite or ProQuest Central. How does the information differ? Which ones are more suitable to use at the beginning stages of your research? How do you know?

Using Databases to Conduct a Good Search

Academic databases offer tools that can make your search much more effective. However, as with any online search, the **output**—your results—are only as good as the **input**—the key words that you provide. Therefore, to make a strong start to your search, you have to think flexibly about the key words in your list. Before looking more deeply into how to use academic databases effectively, do Task 5.2, which is designed to help you to expand your key word list by choosing what you see as the most important keywords and then brainstorming synonyms for them. This will allow you to use the databases to conduct a search that returns more comprehensive, relevant, and valuable results.

Task 5.2

Expanding Your Key Word List to Conduct an Effective Database Search

1. Look at the keyword list you have developed related to your topic. Which synonyms can you use for each key word/phrase? Write each word you are interested in with at least two synonyms. This activity will help you generate more key words for a more effective database search. You can also use a thesaurus to help you (look in Microsoft Word under the Review tab). You can combine all of these words in new ways, which gives you more options for finding relevant results.

Although databases vary according to the amount and type of material that they contain, they generally allow you to do not only a general search, which is similar to a search you would do on the internet using key words, but also an advanced search. An advanced search allows you to use tools that can make your search much more efficient—that is, to find relevant sources more quickly.

An advanced search allows you to pinpoint the type of source you want to refine the search using specific tools, including (1) Boolean searches and (2) limiters.

Tool 1: Boolean Search

When conducting a Boolean search, you use specific commands to tell a search engine what to look for and how. The first way to do a good Boolean search is to use relevant search terms. These can be key words or publication information, such as the author or title. The key word list you already have is useful at this point. For a one-word term, type in the word—for example, ethics. For a phrase of two or more words together, put quotation marks around the phrase so that the words will be searched for as one unit (you can also do this for one-word terms), as in "biodiversity loss."

The next way to get a good Boolean search is to use **Boolean Operators.** The words AND, NOT, and OR are the Boolean operators. They can be used to combine your search terms in different ways to tell the search engine what is important in your search.

- **AND: Limits** your search by looking for documents containing **all** of the key words connected with it. In the example of *susatainability AND "biodiversity loss" AND management,* you will get documents with **all three** terms in it, looking for "biodiversity loss" as one unit (not as separate words).

- **NOT: Excludes** terms that might be commonly used in conjunction with your focus term and **limits** your search by looking for the first term you list and not the terms following NOT, as in *"biodiversity loss" NOT "extinction."*
  - Use NOT in this case if you are not interested in extinction. It saves time because you do not have to weed out documents focusing on extinction as the search itself will do it for you. Note that if you limit the search in this way and you change your topic later to include extinction, you will have to conduct a new search to get relevant documents.
- **OR: Includes** synonyms of your search terms, **expands** your search by allowing you to include terms that are commonly interchanged in the field, and **allows** you to find relevant sources that you might otherwise miss, as in *"biodiversity loss" OR "lack of biodiversity."*

Two special ways to use terms in a Boolean search include parentheses ( ) and a star *. The ( ) group items in a Boolean search. The * conducts a search for all forms of a word.

- Combining operators with ( ): **Limits** search by making it more precise. Parentheses are used to group terms like in math, as in *(sustainability not conservation)* and *("biodiversity loss" or "lack of biodiversity")*.
- Listing * after part of a word to capture all forms (truncation) with *: **Expands** search by allowing you to capture all forms of a word, as in *sustaina**. This will look for *sustainable, sustainability, sustainably,* etc. In an example of *sustainability and manag**, it will look for documents with

the word *sustainability* and any word with the beginning *manag*—*manage, managing, management,* etc. In the example of *sustainability and (ecosystem OR environ*) and (benef* or impact)*, it will look for documents with the word *sustainability* and *ecosystem* or any word with the beginning *environ*—*environment, environmental, ...* and any word beginning with *benef*—*benefit, benefits, beneficial...* or *impact*.

RESEARCH TIP

To facilitate the search process:

- Keep track of your search terms and combinations of terms so that you can go back to the results that you found.
- Keep track of any sources that you find that look relevant so that you can go back to them.
- Use a Word document in which to copy the title and author of papers.
- If you are in an EBSCO database, store the files you find in a folder. Look at other available tools as well, such as the email feature that allows you to email the article to yourself. Talk with a librarian for more information.

<u>Most Important</u>: Always keep track of the search terms and combinations that you use for future reference as your topic/paper develops.

Task 5.3

Conducting a Boolean Search

1. Choose the key terms that you are most interested in. What are six Boolean search strings that you could use for your topic? Use AND and OR at least one time each. Use * and ( ) at least once as well.

    Model answer for topic recycling

    plastic AND recycling
    plastic AND recycling AND (impact or effect)
    plastic AND "negative effect" AND environment
    recycl* AND advantage
    recycl* AND (reason or motivat*)
    recycl* AND "positive effect"
    recycl* AND econ*

2. Do a Boolean search using some of these strings in at least two different databases. Which three sources from these databases might be useful for your paper? Record the database and search terms you used. Record the bibliographic information for each, using the citation style that is preferred in your field or required in most of your classes: MLA? APA? other?

    Model answer for topic recycling

    Search terms used: *plastic AND recycling AND (impact OR effect)*

    Citation:
    Haider, T. P., Völker, C., Kramm, J., Landfester, K., & Wurm, F. R. (2019). Plastics of the Future? The impact of biodegradable polymers on the environment and on society. *Angewandte Chemie International Edition, 58*(1), 50–62. https://doi.org/10.1002/anie.201805766

3. After this process, how have your ideas about your research topic changed? What further refining of your topic might be possible? Perform an analysis similar to the model.

   Model answer for topic recycling

   I was able to narrow the topic to be more suitable for a 10- to 12-page paper. I should be able to provide the right amount of detailed support for the narrowed topic within the 10- to 12-page space. I narrowed by

   1) not covering all of recycling, but one specific type: recycling of plastic.
   2) I'm going to focus on its effects, not what it is or the process or other aspects. Depending on what I find, I may narrow it down to specific effects -- not as general as "effects of recycling on the environment," or to one effect that I will explore more deeply.

4. What biases (see Lesson 4) did you notice? How do you plan to lessen the impact of bias on your research?

   I recognized some bias in my key words as I created my Boolean strings—I was choosing words that only looked at the benefits of recycling, which would make the paper biased in that direction, so I chose some words that will allow me to find sources that may have a different point of view. I will continue to review each step I take for bias and remember that I have this bias to help me write a paper that is less biased and more comprehensive on the topic.

Tool 2: Limiters

The other way to limit the number of sources that you find to make the search more effective is to use limiters. **Limiters** are found in most academic databases. They allow you refine your search in various ways such as by source and document type, scholarly/peer-reviewed, date, or full text.

1. Source/Document Type

When you use this limiter, consider the characteristics of the different types or format (book, magazine, etc.) of sources as related to your course, your topic, and the requirements of the assignment (see Table 5.1).

TABLE 5.1
Source and Document Formats and Types

Publication/Source Format	Document Type
Book	Article
Journal Article	Bibliography
Magazine Article	Abstract
Organization/White Paper	Book Chapter
Trade Publication (a periodical written for an audience in a certain field/trade)	Review
Audio/Video	Primary Source Document (works of art, speeches, etc)
Image	Film
Others	Others

2. Scholarly/Peer-Reviewed

This limiter allows you to choose to see only those sources that have been peer-reviewed, meaning they have been read and approved by experts in the field as being valuable and valid.

3. Date

This allows you to limit your results to items published in a certain time period. This is especially valuable if you are only looking for recent research.

4. Full Text Only/PDF Full Text

This allows you to limit the results to those that have full text in the database. If you don't limit to full text only, you will get more results, but some of them may not be available through your library in this particular database.

However, it is often better to not limit to full text only. This is because even if the full text is not available through this database, you can click a phrase like "Find It" that you may see on your screen by the name of the source, and the library website will indicate whether you can get it through another database that the library has access to or through interlibrary loan (your university library will request it from another library for you).

Other common limiters are language, journal name, publisher, company, and location.

You can sometimes find a list of limiters to choose from when you enter the Advanced Search of a database. They are also usually available on the left side of the screen once you have a list of sources from a search. Each database is a little different, so you will have to explore a little. The best place to start is your university library's research guides (often organized by discipline).

Task 5.4

Comparing Characteristics of Databases

Answer the questions for at least two databases on the list or databases that you know you will be using in your field.

Academic Search Premier/Elite   ProQuest Central   JSTOR   SCOPUS

LexisNexis Academic   Web of Science   ERIC   Other?

	Database	Database
1. When you click on Advanced Search, do you see a list of limiters? If so, what the categories do you see?		
2. Do a search for "sustainability AND environment."		
▪ How many sources do you get?		
▪ List each of the different types of sources found and the number of each. (Hint: Look on the left side of the page.)		

3. Limit your search to Journals (Academic/Scholarly/etc). Click on the first article. If you see something called "details," click on it. Do you see: the author's name?		
• a link to more information about the author?		
• other publication information? If so, what type(s)?		
• a way to get a citation for the article? How do you get the citation?		
• subject headings that the article falls under? What are they?		
• a doi number (a digital identifier for this article)? What is it?		
• What other important details do you see about the article?		
• What other important tasks can you do from this screen (e.g., send an email, get PDF, save the article to a folder)?		

Lesson Connection

Review the information and tasks in this lesson. Write a paragraph that includes:

- *what* you learned in this particular lesson.
- *how* it is significant for you.
- *why* it is important for you to know.

Be sure to consider: *Which* information/activities were most valuable for you and *why*? How might you use this information in the future?

LESSON 6

Reading with Purpose: The Structure of a Research Article

Now that you have some possible sources for your assignment, use them as starting points to deepen and expand your research. Read them to begin finding out what will work for your research.

To conduct research more efficiently, you need to read quickly to get a general idea of the content, called **skimming,** and read to find specific information, called **scanning.** To skim and scan effectively, you need to know where to look within a source to find information that could be valuable to you.

The Structure of a Research Article

Knowing how research articles are organized can help you at two points in the research process:

1. When conducting research: Knowing what type of information can be found where will help you to scan articles more quickly for key words and to skim for information related to your topic that you might want to incorporate as outside source information.

2. When writing your paper: You will become familiar with academic writing conventions regarding typical structure and expected content, which will help you structure your own paper.

In most disciplines, academic articles that report on a specific study and its results follow a common structure to make it easier for the reader to find information quickly. Some people refer to this structure as IMRD, as shown in Figure 6.1.

If the article is not reporting on primary research (see Lesson 7), it may not have this structure. In this case, it will follow another **rhetorical pattern**, such as

- describing a process.
- listing causes or effects.
- doing a comparison or contrast.
- listing advantages or disadvantages.

FIGURE 6.1
Typical Structure of an Article Reporting Primary Research

Abstract
→ a basic overview of the content of the article
- the problem addressed
- how the authors studied the problem
- what they found
- possible implications

Introduction/Literature Review (I)
→ explanation of the basic context being explored
- definition/explanation of key ideas
- what previous researchers have said
- significance of understanding this topic better
- objectives of this research/gap filled in the literature

Methodology (M)
→ explanation of methods used
- participants and variables in the study
- data collection methods
- data analysis methods

Results (R)
→ presentation of results of the study
- summary of the data found
- figures and tables that present data visually

Discussion (D)
→ discussion of the significance of results found
- how results fit within context of what others have found
- how these results contribute to the research
- implications of results for practice
- ideas for future research
- strengths and limitations of this study

Conclusion (optional)
→ if present, significance of results in a broader context and plans for future work

References/Bibliography
→ list of sources referred to in the main text

Strategies for Reading Research

Once you are familiar with the structure of a research article and the type of information that is typically found in each section, you will be able to read more efficiently and quickly. Some strategies to keep in mind are shown in Figure 6.2.

Remember, at this point, you are <u>not</u> reading the whole article and you are <u>not</u> reading to understand all of the information. You are **skimming** and **scanning** to find information that will tell you if the article has information related to your research. The ultimate goal as you skim articles you have found is to: (1) identify sources that fit with your topic and (2) eliminate sources that do not fit with your topic. Therefore, do not spend time trying to understand everything. Instead, focus on finding key words and phrases that are related to your research and that tell you what the author is doing in each section.

FIGURE 6.2
Strategies for Efficient Reading of a Research Article

• Skim the abstract first. Is it related?	Yes—continue into the article. No—take it off of your ongoing list of sources.
• Identify the structure (or rhetorical pattern).	Use this information to guide you to the most important sections.
• Look in the Introduction for more related literature that you might want to look at for your own research.	You can find the bibliographic information in the source list at the end of the paper for anything that looks relevant.
• If it is reporting on primary research, look in the Discussion and Conclusion sections for more key words and ideas that you might agree or disagree with.	These ideas will help you to develop your own argument and critical thinking on the topic.
• Note any new key words/ideas and sources you have found and use them to continue to deepen your search.	Don't be afraid to move out from your original sources and make your own connections among related ideas to get a better sense of the shape of content and ideas that are part of the conversation. You may want to create new idea maps or add to one you've already created (see pp. 27–31). This will improve the quality of your knowledge and the value of your research project.

Task 6.1

Reading to Find Useful Information

Now practice reading for useful information for the topic you have chosen.

First, use your key word list and Boolean strings from previous lessons to find three possible academic articles that might be useful for your own research. Then, skim the abstract and headings of each and eliminate any that do not seem to fit. If none seem useful, do another search. Finally, when you find one that seems useful, answer these questions to help you develop your own ideas further.

1. Look at the abstract. What sentences do the author(s) use to identify the main organization/topics covered in the article?

2. Look at the headings to clarify how the article is organized so readers can find things more efficiently.

3. Look in the Discussion and Conclusion sections for more key words and ideas that you might agree or disagree with.

4. What are three sources from the references section in this article that seem like they might be useful for your research?

5. Find these articles and skim their abstracts. Which one(s) will you take a closer look at? Why?

6. What new ideas/directions for research did you get from the article(s)? How do the new ideas fit with the ideas you already have?

Bias in the Process of Reading

Now that you have begun looking at article content, bias may enter in again in the form of cherry picking. Also known as **issue bias, cherry picking** occurs when you (consciously or unconsciously) pick and choose which information to use from an article based on whether it supports your point of view or not and/or ignore the information that does not support your point of view. An example is shown:

> Example 1:
>> Original text:
>> We observed a robust correlation between higher levels of gun ownership and higher firearm homicide rates. Although we could not determine causation, we found that states with higher rates of gun ownership had disproportionately large numbers of deaths from firearm-related homicides.
>
>> from abstract of Siegel, Michael, M.D., M.P.H., Ross, C. S., M.B.A., & King, Charles, III, J.D., PhD. (2013). The relationship between gun ownership and firearm homicide rates in the United States, 1981–2010. *American Journal of Public Health, 103*(11), 2098-2105. Retrieved from https://search-proquest-com.authenticate.library.duq.edu/docview/1448191039?accountid=10610

If you cherry pick by just using the first sentence, readers might assume a causal relationship. However, the statement *Although we could not determine causation* reveals that this is not true. You need to include the second sentence to not mislead your reader.

Here is another example.

> Example 2:
> Original text:
> Ramsey Clark, former United States Attorney General, also ventured into the mire of methodology, but his saving grace is his sociological sophistication. He states, "Not only is the percentage of murders committed by firearms higher in areas where there are more guns and weaker laws—the overall murder rate is higher, too. . . . The inescapable lesson is that easy access to guns causes thousands of preventable murders, suicides and accidental deaths" (1970:104–105). Unfortunately, Clark does not provide us with the source of his conclusion....
>
> from Murray, D. (1975). Handguns, gun control laws and firearm violence. *Social Problems, 23*(1), 81–93. doi:10.2307/799630

You could use the quote from Clark as support in a paper supporting gun control.

> "Not only is the percentage of murders committed by firearms higher in areas where there are more guns and weaker laws—the overall murder rate is higher, too. . . . The inescapable lesson is that easy access to guns causes thousands of preventable murders, suicides and accidental deaths" (1970:104–105).

However, doing so ignores the fact that Clarke does not offer support for this conclusion, making it seem unreliable. You are selecting only the material from sources that support your viewpoint and implying agreement with your stance.

Lesson Connection

Review the information and tasks in this lesson. Write a paragraph that includes:

- *what* you learned in this particular lesson.
- *how* it is significant for you.
- *why* it is important for you to know.

Be sure to consider: *Which* information/activities were most valuable for you and *why*? How might you use this information in the future?

LESSON 7

Authority Is Constructed and Contextual 1: Identifying Source Characteristics

Primary versus Secondary Sources

There are two important concepts that need to be discussed before we delve more into source characteristics. **Primary sources** are direct evidence of an event or direct representation of what you are studying and exist in a variety of formats. Because they are often first-hand accounts, you have to consider that the information provided may be biased or subjective—that is, written from the perspective of someone located in a particular context (place and time). Therefore, while a first-hand account can provide valuable details about the situation, it may not be able to serve as definitive proof.

Currency Place in the Information Cycle

The **information cycle** refers to the progression of types of media coverage that occur after an event happens (the same day of the event, that week, after a few months, …). Knowledge of the information cycle enables you to have an idea of how far from the original event a source is usually published, which typically indicates what kinds of information might be found in a source. This knowledge can make your search for information more comprehensive and effective as information about an event develops as time goes on. Of course, sources can appear at various times in the information cycle, but the basic information cycle is presented in Figure 7.1.

Secondary sources provide an analysis of an event; they do not provide direct evidence because they are at a distance from the origin of the event or item being studied. However, if they are found in a peer-reviewed, academic context such as an academic journal, they can be used as valid support for further analysis.

Task 7.1

Distinguishing between Primary and Secondary Sources

Use the internet to find information about primary and secondary sources. Scribbr.com is one possibility.

1. How do you think primary sources are different from secondary sources according to the website(s) you viewed?

2. What are some possible examples?

3. What are some possible primary sources that might be useful for your research topic?

4. Do you think that one type of source (primary or secondary) might be more valuable than the other for your topic? Explain.

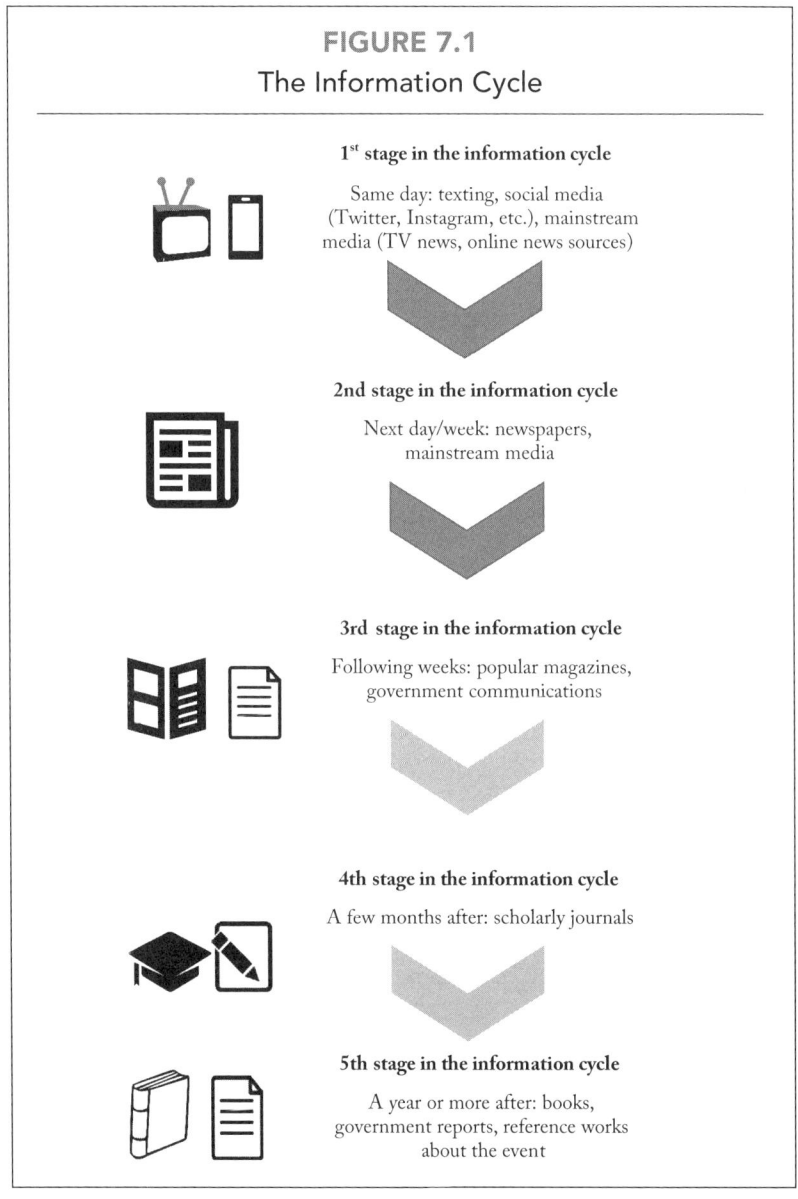

FIGURE 7.1
The Information Cycle

1st stage in the information cycle
Same day: texting, social media (Twitter, Instagram, etc.), mainstream media (TV news, online news sources)

2nd stage in the information cycle
Next day/week: newspapers, mainstream media

3rd stage in the information cycle
Following weeks: popular magazines, government communications

4th stage in the information cycle
A few months after: scholarly journals

5th stage in the information cycle
A year or more after: books, government reports, reference works about the event

The value of a source in the information cycle is shown in Table 7.1

TABLE 7.1
The Value of a Source in the Information Cycle

Place in the Information Cycle	Information Found	Possible Biases
Same day (texts, social media, mainstream media)	Provides immediate news; offers a variety of perspectives from those who were there.	**Emotional content:** Reports are often from individuals at the scene, which means the information is being presented from the viewpoint of individuals who are still reacting emotionally to events that have just happened and who may have played a part in the actual event. This results in personal bias. **Gaps in information:** Many facts may still be missing at this stage, meaning the information is not comprehensive. Not having a complete picture also contributes to bias.
Next day/week of (newspapers, mainstream media)	Presents facts of what happened as they appear; fills in gaps in information about an event.	**Selection bias:** The mainstream media may have an agenda that influences their choices with respect to content and positioning of the facts.
Following weeks (popular magazines, government communications)	Provides more facts about the event; more personal stories and debate provided; how is the story seen in the social and political arenas?	**Emotional content:** Popular magazines tend to print personal perspectives, which are sometimes emotionally charged and therefore biased. **Selection bias:** Government communications and others may also only present information that promotes a particular political, social, or economic agenda.
A few months/1 or 2 years after (scholarly journals)	Presents results from primary research related to the event to explore it more deeply to see cause-and-effect relationships and create a better understanding; includes analysis of the event from different journals and allows for analysis from different perspectives.	**Credible and accurate.** In general, these are peer-reviewed and so the quality should be good in terms of credibility and accuracy of content. **Selection bias:** You still should look at interpretation of the event in a few journals to get a variety of perspectives because not all studies get the same results so bias can still be an issue. The more sources you consult, the more comprehensive your view and the better you can determine bias.
A year or more after (books, government reports, reference works about the event)	Offers a variety of types of information about the event in a variety of formats; more time has passed since the event, so the content tends to be more analytical and less personal in nature.	**Agenda Bias:** These can promote a particular personal or political agenda.

Identifying Source Characteristics

Lessons 7 and 8 teach you how to use the *wh-* questions (*who, what, when, where, why*) typically used for analysis as criteria for evaluating sources. It will show you how to apply them in two ways: (1) to perform a **surface** analysis to identify the characteristics of a source (Lesson 7) and (2) to perform a **deeper** analysis to investigate the appropriateness of a source for use in academic research (Lesson 8). The order in which you will deal with them will be: *why, where, when, who, what.*

The characteristics of a source are important to recognize because the quality of each characteristic influences the **credibility, reliability,** and/or **validity** of the source. For an academic research project, for example, you would not want to use a source where credibility, reliability, or validity might be called into question because this would raise questions about your own research capabilities and lower the quality of your research product. Note that because unsubstantiated claims are so common in the information sources we read every day, such an analysis is also useful to perform in your everyday life.

The first step in evaluating the information in a source is to identify the characteristics of a source. What can the source tell you about the information? By identifying the characteristics of a source, you are performing an **objective** analysis. At this point, you are not interpreting the information in any way—you are merely listing it for your references.

Table 7.2 presents a breakdown of the basic characteristics of a source that you must be able to identify to perform the subjective analysis that follows effectively. It's important to become familiar with a variety of formats to improve your ability to efficiently and effectively conduct a source evaluation.

TABLE 7.2
Source Characteristics

Where	
Context of source (type of publication)	<ul><li>website</li><li>newspaper</li><li>book</li><li>trade publication</li><li>white paper (published report by a government, non-profit organization, or corporation)</li><li>scholarly journal</li></ul>
When	
When it was published	<ul><li>recently</li><li>a few years ago</li><li>many years ago</li></ul>
When it appears in the information cycle	<ul><li>while the event is occurring, same day</li><li>immediately after the event, same week</li><li>a few weeks after the event</li><li>a few months to a year or two after the event</li><li>one to several years after the event</li></ul>
Who	
Author background/ qualifications	<ul><li>non-professional individual</li><li>journalist</li><li>scholar/expert</li></ul>
Publisher/ Sponsor/ Promoter	<ul><li>commercial company</li><li>news organization</li><li>professional society or organization publication</li><li>academic journal</li></ul>
What (Content)	
Appearance	<ul><li>Title and presentation of several general paragraphs on a topic are included; no subheadings.</li><li>Photographs accompany text without explanation in the text.</li><li>General subheadings are included that generally indicate the topic of the text that follows.</li><li>Subheadings are included that indicate more specifically the purpose of text that follows.</li><li>Charts and figures are included to clarify concepts and are explained in detail in the text.</li></ul>
Type of information	<ul><li>general description</li><li>personal narrative</li><li>quotes from interviews</li><li>citations</li><li>explanation of formal, field-related processes or concepts</li><li>statistics</li><li>charts</li><li>figures</li><li>photographs</li><li>a references section that lists sources</li></ul>
Language	<ul><li>Written in language the general public can understand.</li><li>Written in language the general public can understand, but may use professional jargon.</li><li>Written in scholarly language that requires some knowledge of concepts in the field.</li></ul>
Edited/ Peer-reviewed	<ul><li>Content has not been edited.</li><li>Content has been edited by a general editor (such as with a newspaper or magazine).</li><li>Content has been judged to be high quality by experts in the field who have read it and provided comments.</li></ul>

Task 7.2

Investigating the Characteristics of a Source

Using the information in Table 7.1, review two sources to identify the where, when, who, and what for each. What questions or concerns do you have?

Accessibility of Sources and Bias

Be aware that some information that you find may be open and free to you, and some will be behind a paywall, meaning you must pay a fee to access the information (see Table 7.3).

Many high-quality sources (peer-reviewed/edited) are behind a paywall. Typically those attending or working at universities or members of professional groups can access this type of source, but others cannot. Lack of access to some types of sources can lead to bias in a research product as all perspectives may not be considered in the analysis or represented. This is why it is important to consider "type of information" under **What.**

Be sure to carefully consider the characteristics of the sources that you choose to include in your research. Use the information in this lesson as you do your research to help you improve the quality of your research.

TABLE 7.3
Accessibility of Sources

Access Is Free	Must Pay a Fee to Read
• books at the library	• scholarly journal sources
• some news sources	• some news sources
• some magazines	• some magazines
• some trade journals	• some trade journals
• information on many websites: company, non-profit, government websites	

> **RESEARCH TIP**
>
> Sometimes you cannot find an author for a website because a general member of the staff of an organization wrote it. In this case, consider the organization itself to be the author.

Lesson Connection

Review the information and tasks in this lesson. Write a paragraph that includes:

- *what* you learned in this particular lesson.
- *how* it is significant for you.
- *why* it is important for you to know.

Be sure to consider: *Which* information/activities were most valuable for you and *why*? How might you use this information in the future?

LESSON 8

Authority Is Constructed and Contextual 2: Examining Source Characteristics and Bias to Determine Appropriateness

Examining source characteristics allows you to determine a source's **appropriateness** for use in academic research. A source that is appropriate has **credibility, reliability,** and **validity**. When you evaluate source characteristics, you must also consider **bias**. This means you have to examine how the **opinion, perspective,** or **prejudice** of those involved in the publication of the source (the *who*), as well as intended audience and purpose (the *why*), may have influenced choices with respect to the content.

Table 8.1 provides some ways to think about the appropriateness of your sources, which is information that will help you decide whether to keep this source and perform a more comprehensive analysis. The information provided in Table 8.1 is a suggestion. You will need to look at all the characteristics of a source and how that information may interact when determining a source's appropriateness. Conventions vary according to field too, which also impacts how one can judge appropriateness.

TABLE 8.1
Some Ways to Think about the Appropriateness of Sources

	Most Likely Appropriate	Possibly Appropriate	Most Likely Not Appropriate
why (purpose)	to inform	to persuade	• to sell something • to present personal opinion • to promote a particular political agenda
where (context)	• scholarly/peer reviewed • scholarly/not peer-reviewed • .gov or .edu website • trade publication • newspaper	.com .org	social media
when	up-to-date information	not current but still has valuable historical or background information	when new information makes the information in your source irrelevant, you should not use it
who	expert in the field journalist	professional writer	non-professional writer
what (content)	• comprehensive coverage of a topic • facts and statistics • charts and graphs • photographs • citations	commentary on an issue personal narrative	

The table uses *wh-* questions as a way to perform a deeper evaluation. *Why* establishes a foundation for your evaluation of the other characteristics (see Figure 8.1), which is why it comes first. *Why* is followed by *where* and *when* because if a source was not published in a credible or reliable place or the date of publication is not acceptable for your topic, then you do not need to consider it any longer. Tools for conducting a deeper analysis are provided after the table.

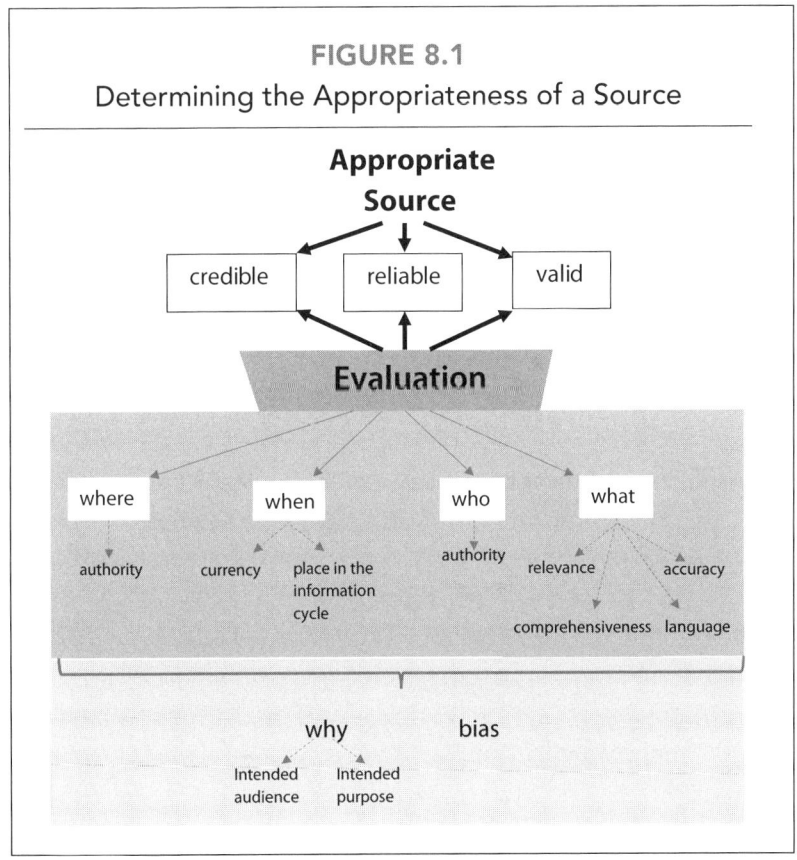

FIGURE 8.1
Determining the Appropriateness of a Source

Tools to help you consider each characteristic to determine appropriateness are provided with application tasks for your sources. Choose a few of the sources you have found to use for each of the tasks. Doing each task for just one source can be helpful as practice; however, because each source has its own individual characteristics, completing each task for three or more sources will allow you to compare sources, which will make your evaluation more complete.

Considering the *Why* to Recognize Bias

As you consider the where, when, who and what of a source, remember that the *why* underlies all of the choices made by those involved in the publishing of the source. It can affect each characteristic of the source and sometimes lead to bias. Considering the *why* includes thinking about the intended audience and purpose of those involved in the writing and publishing of the source. Ask yourself:

- Is the intended audience made up of scholars in the field? college-educated readers? any adult reader?
- Does the author want to inform the reader? Persuade the reader? sell the reader something? present an opinion or viewpoint?

As you conduct your evaluation of the source, you must keep in mind the author's intentions and how they influence choices about where to publish and what to include (or not). Allow your decision about the author's intended audience and purpose guide you as you consider the *where, when, who,* and *what* of each source.

Task 8.1

Examining the Why

As you evaluate each source, continue to consider these questions.

1. What is the author's intended audience?

2. What is the author's intended purpose?

Determining the Appropriateness of *Where*: Assessing Authority

To determine the appropriateness of the context, you must consider what authority the publication—the journal, news source, web site—has and what possible biases it may have. These biases impact the quality of the information and the choices made about what to include. If a website is a .gov or .edu, the information is probably more authoritative and has less bias than the information found on a .com site. This is because the author of a .gov or .edu likely has strong qualifications to write about the topic and the publisher is less likely to have an agenda to promote. However, be aware that bias is never entirely lacking. A .gov or .edu may also promote a particular agenda as well, determined by political ideology or the stated mission of the site. It is up to you to do your research to ensure the credibility, reliability and validity of the information you use as support in your research.

Task 8.2

Examining the Where

Apply what you have learned about how to evaluate the where of a source to at least three of the sources you have found for your research.

Determining the Appropriateness of *When*: Assessing Currency and Place in the Information Cycle

How current the information is influences the appropriateness of your source. Refer back to the Information Cycle in Lesson 7. Information about an event becomes more comprehensive as information about an event evolves over time. If you are using a source for background or historical context, the information will be credible and reliable whether or not it is recent. If you are using statistical data from the source, however, you must be sure that it is up-to-date.

To achieve credibility in many fields, you must have the most up-to-date information, which means that your sources should not be more than about three years old. Think about your research topic and determine the cut-off year for information that is valuable for you.

Task 8.3

Examining the When

Apply what you have learned about how to evaluate the when of a source to at least three of the sources you have found for your research.

Determining the Appropriateness of *Who*: Assessing Authority

It is essential to consider the authority and the possible biases of those who are involved in the publication of the source. For example, an article written by someone who has written several articles on the same topic and is the leader in a related professional organization will probably have authority. At the same time, who that person is affiliated with, such as professional organizations and workplaces, can mean that this person has adopted a particular perspective, which influences content and leads to bias. Table 8.2 provides some qualifications for you to use when analyzing for authority.

TABLE 8.2

Criteria for Determining the Appropriateness of Who

The Author	The Publisher	The Sponsor/Promoter
- education - work context - experience in the field - number of previous publications on this topic - organizations he/she is a member of - reputation	- age of the publishing company - impact factor of journal (how often it is cited) - reputation - mission statement	- reputation - mission statement - connections to other organizations

Some criteria to help you evaluate the credibility and reliability of the author are listed.

- Is the author well-educated on this topic?
- Does the author have research experience/history in this area?
- Does the author have other publications on this topic?
- Does the author belong to organizations that might bias their perspective?
- Is the author well-known in the field or for knowledge/expertise in the topic area?

RESEARCH TIP

You will have to search for information about *who* online. If you are using an academic database, the detailed record often provides links to more information about the author and the journal in which the article can be found. Otherwise, a general online search can also provide information.

Sample Evaluation of *Who*

A sample analysis of the author's credibility is provided. The article used is on the topic of the sustainability of the use of plastic and can be found at https://onlinelibrary.wiley.com/doi/full/10.1002/anie.201805766. You don't need the article to follow along.

> Haider, T. P., Völker, C., Kramm, J., Landfester, K., & Wurm, F. R. (2018). Plastics of the Future? The Impact of Biodegradable Polymers on the Environment and on Society. *Angewandte Chemie International Edition, 58*(1), 50-62. doi:10.1002/anie.201805766

Facts about the Authors

> The first author, Tobias P. Haider, works at the Max Planck Institute for Polymer Research, which, according to expert science reviews online, is one of the best research centers in this area worldwide. He has a Master of Science degree in Chemistry. He has written several other articles in this area and has been cited by many.
>
> The second author, Carolin Volker—along with the third author, Johanna Kramm—works at the Institute for Social-Ecological Research, which focuses on promoting transdisciplinary sustainability research. Both also have an impressive bibliography. Their group, the junior research group PlastX, is "examining the societal role of plastic and the associated environmental impacts. Within this framework, the team of social and natural scientists is attempting to find out how plastic might be used more sustainably" (https://www.isoe.de/en/research/junior-research-group/).
>
> **The qualifications of these authors means they do have the authority to write about this topic.**

Analysis of Authority and Biases

The qualifications of these authors indicate they have the expertise and authority to write about the topic. Their beliefs about the need for sustainability and their dependence on funding could influence their methodology, results, or interpretation of results, leading them to increase the likelihood of obtaining outcomes that reflect those beliefs or further funding. Specifically, this paper calls for development of biodegradable plastics, citing the need for this because of problems caused by plastic garbage worldwide. As these researchers study polymers and plastics, their support for the development of biodegradable plastics could be a result of their own interests—personal and financial.

Facts about the Publisher

Angewandte Chemie is a journal of the German Chemical Society. This journal has a high impact factor, meaning it is frequently cited by others.

Analysis of Authority and Biases

This journal seems to offer information on a wide variety of topics and be very professional. Because it is not limited in scope, it seems likely it is not biased.

Facts about the Sponsors/Promoters

In this case, the publisher is also the sponsor—the German Chemical Society. Often, associations or societies are professional organizations that are credentialed in a specific field and have to meet field standards, so they are credible.

Analysis of Authority and Biases

A "society" would tend to be in support of the field or discipline so it is likely not biased.

Task 8.4

Examining the Who

Apply what you have learned about how to evaluate the who of a source to at least three of the sources you have found for your research.

Determining the Appropriateness of *What* (Content): Assessing Relevance, Accuracy, and Comprehensiveness

Of course, in this whole source evaluation process, you are looking for sources that match your topic and are current and accurate.

Some questions to ask regarding **relevance** are:

- Is it appropriate for the context that you are writing about?
- How does it fit in the conversation?
- Which part of your discussion does it support?
- Does it share the same audience that your research will?

The validity of your research depends on the accuracy of the sources that you use as references. Table 8.3 provides some questions to ask and strategies for discovering the answers to the questions.

TABLE 8.3
Explaining the What: Accuracy

Questions to Ask to Determine Accuracy	Strategies for Discovering the Answers
• Where did the information in the source come from? • Does the source cite valid sources on the same topic? • When was it published? • When were its references published?	• Look up some of the references and their authors, content, etc. • Look at any primary research. • Look at the dates of publication and information about when the primary research was conducted.
• Does the research process seem valid?	• Ask a professor or other expert in your field to help you.
• Was the information in the source reviewed by experts to verify authenticity?	• Look for evidence the source was peer-reviewed or refereed.

A source lacks **comprehensiveness** when it presents information that is limited in scope—that is, that does not provide a thorough look at all sides. Perhaps some facts are not reported or others are reported using language to promote a one perspective. Limitations in terms of accessibility (see p. 73) may have influenced the information available to the author, which would limit the research scope of the source. It's also possible that statistical analyses may not consider all variables, thereby skewing results. A lack of comprehensiveness causes bias. Let your knowledge of the topic guide you in your analysis. If necessary, ask a professor or other expert to help you evaluate the statistical analysis.

Evaluation of *What* Regarding Relevance, Accuracy, and Comprehensiveness

A sample analysis of the source's value is provided using the same article on biodegradable polymers.

Relevance

> This article is appropriate to use for my research because I want to write about the ubiquitous use of plastic in our everyday lives and how we need to make plastics more sustainable to prevent the build-up of garbage on our planet, which causes pollution problems. This article has scientific facts/information that I can use for support.

> This article is appropriate for my expected audience of college-educated readers. It provides statistical support for the idea that more real-world testing is needed to determine the biodegradability of plastics being used. While it is scientific, it is a little easier to read than a report of primary research in this area would be.

Accuracy

> Of the 88 sources cited, most are from scientific journals in chemistry, biology, environmental science, etc. A few are government documents. The journals are peer-reviewed and edited, so the information should be trustworthy. The source cites valid sources that explore the same topic. For example [76] is a report by the Environmental Protection Agency of the U.S. government. The website offers an explanation of the methodology used to get their numbers on materials, waste, and recycling in the U.S.

The journal has an editorial board and an International Advisory Board that give input on content. The information was peer-reviewed.

Currency

The publication dates for the references range from the 1990s to 2018. Background information is often more historical, which is where the earlier sources are useful. The newer sources provide the science facts for the paper. Both are useful for my topic. This was written in 2019, so it is current. The science and the context with respect to plastic use and laws restricting its use are current, meaning there have not been changes that make this paper's conclusion irrelevant. There is a Check for Updates note on the page online, but the data on updates was not available when I clicked on it.

Comprehensiveness

From the research I have done, it seems that information in the article covers the main topics in the conversation about plastics. The number and variety of sources used as references also indicate that this article is comprehensive.

Task 8.5

Examining the What

Apply what you have learned about how to evaluate the what of a source to at least three of the sources you have found for your research.

Performing a Complete Evaluation of a Source

An example of one way to complete an evaluation of a source is provided. You will do it yourself in Task 8.6.

Example Complete Evaluation

1. *Publication Information*

Title: Science of learning: Why do we care?

Authors: Helyn Kim, Eileen McGivney, and Esther Care

Publication date: Tuesday, March 28, 2017

Publisher: Brookings

URL (if a website): https://www.brookings.edu/blog/education-plus-development/2017/03/28/science-of-learning-why-do-we-care/

Database found in (if database was used): X

2. *Why: Audience/Purpose*

Who was this written for? How do you know (look at appearance, language, structure of the piece, writing style, references)? Provide two or three sentences to support your ideas.

> This seems to have been written to help people in education who are interested in the changes in education and how the science of learning can inform us about how to teach better.
>
> Probably for teachers.
>
> Has a lot of explanation, which means the readers may not be familiar with some of the concepts. Fairly simple language.

Structure is simple like an essay. You can click on many links to get more information. Some of the links are more scientific. There is no References section, but the links act as references.

Seems mostly for background information. Not a lot of technical information.

Language/word choice is fairly objective.

Example Language:

"In addition to answering these questions about skills development and learning, we need to explore…"

"A recent OECD report finds that research on learning does not consistently inform the everyday practice of teachers, showing a further divide between learning sciences and schooling. To no fault of teachers, the science of learning is often not translated into digestible and practical strategies."

3. *Who: Determining Authority*

Who wrote the article? What qualifications do he/she/they have to write on this topic and how do they qualify the author? Who published/sponsored/promoted the article?

What are potential biases of the author/publisher/sponsor? How is this a bias?

Author(s)

Helyn Kim

Postdoctoral Fellow—Global Economy and Development, Center for Universal Education

Dr. Kim received her PhD in Education from the University of Virginia. Her doctoral work provided a multi-dimensional approach to understanding the nature and interplay among the foundations of learning and development in school-aged children.

Eileen McGivney

> Former Research Associate—Center for Universal Education
>
> Dr. McGivney has done a lot of research and written many articles about education.

Esther Care

> Senior Fellow—Global Economy and Development, Center for Universal Education
>
> Dr. Care is very involved in educational research and directs centers that do research and try to improve education.

Publisher/Sponsor/Promoter: Brookings

> The Brookings Institution is a nonprofit public policy organization based in Washington, DC. Its mission is to conduct in-depth research that leads to new ideas for solving problems facing society at the local, national, and global level.

Possible Biases of Each

> The authors may be biased if they have done a lot of research from one perspective of education – that may make them unwilling to see other perspectives. But they don't necessarily have any bias. They are professionals who have much experience and done a lot of research so they are educated and should be good at critical analysis, which should help them avoid bias.
>
> The publisher is a non-profit, so it is not out to make money by promoting a specific point of view. However, if the donors who give them money have a certain perspective, they may feel pressure to support that perspective in what they publish.

4. *What: Determining relevance, accuracy and comprehensiveness*
What key words or ideas fit with your research? How do they fit?

> I am writing a paper on the science of learning and how it can inform teaching. Some matching key words and phrases: *science of learning, how to teach skills, multiple pathways for learning, transferring what we know about learning to the classroom.*

Where did the information in the article come from—what references/sources are used for support? Are they valid? Do they have any biases?

> Some of the references are more general like TED talks or from organizations in education. Others are other articles written by each of the authors, sometimes with a different author. Everyone who works at Brookings is an expert, so the information in the article has been written by professionals. It does not seem overtly biased, but because some of the references are other articles written by the same authors, it may promote their perspective rather than having a complete view.
>
> This article seems to contain a lot of links to reputable sources that will have even more information for me.

Has the source been peer-reviewed?

> No.

Is there comprehensive coverage of the topic? Does it cover all aspects of it or is the content biased to support the author's perspective? Think carefully about what *comprehensive* means with respect to this topic and provide evidence to support your answer.

> As I mentioned, they cite themselves, but they also bring in others as support for their point of view in the conclusion that "Uncovering the progression of skills, studying how governments identify effective practices and scale them up, and determining what works best for teachers to support

their knowledge and practice are all areas where we can do a better job of learning about both the *why* and the *how*."

They ask a lot of questions in the article for people to think about. They don't promote one course of action, but suggest various things to consider and various ways to address the issue of needing more research about how knowing more about the science of learning can benefit education.

Therefore, it seems fairly comprehensive. I would definitely use links to other sources provided to further explore the ideas on the website, which are somewhat basic.

Summary of article evaluation:

Write a brief summary (at least 8 sentences) summarizing what you have found out about this source. Write about information that is important for clarifying how it is good and how it is not so good. In what situation would this be a good source to use? When would it NOT be a good source to use? Why?

This source seems like a good one to use if I am writing about how the science of learning can inform how we teach. The authors are experts and the Brookings Institute is a famous non-profit that funds expert research in many areas, so bias does not seem to be an issue. The article provides valid, current references to get a broader perspective. The language is approachable for most readers and yet the topic is scientific and research support is offered if someone wants to read more. I would definitely be able to use this as a source and/or use some of the references as sources for a paper. I will continue to compare the information I find in various sources to evaluate for bias and ensure comprehensiveness of my discussion.

Task 8.6

Evaluating a Source

Perform a complete evaluation for one source that you have found. Use the information in this lesson and the example presented to guide you.

Lesson Connection

Review the information and tasks in this lesson. Write a paragraph that includes:

- *what* you learned in this particular lesson.
- *how* it is significant for you.
- *why* it is important for you to know.

Be sure to consider: *Which* information/activities were most valuable for you and *why*? How might you use this information in the future?

Appendix A: Information Literacy Skills and the Research Cycle

An integration of the information literacy skills into the steps of the research cycle (presented in Lesson 1) is shown. The lesson number that each skills corresponds with is in ( ).

- **Research Cycle Step 1: Develop questions.**

    Information literacy skills—identify information gaps (1), find key words for a search (2), create idea map (3), avoid confirmation bias (4).

- **Research Cycle Step 2: Find sources that can answer these questions.**

    Information literacy skills—use databases (5), use Boolean search and limiters (5).

- **Research Cycle Step 3: Read sources.**

    Information literacy skills—find information in a research article (6), avoid selection bias/cherry picking (6), evaluate sources (7 and 8).

- **Research Cycle Step 4: Get new ideas.**

    Information Literacy skills—find information in a research article (6), add to key words for a search (2), revise idea map (3).

- **Research Cycle Step 5: Do a refined search.**

    Information literacy skills—use databases (5), use Boolean search and limiters (5).

- **Research Cycle Step 6: Fit new ideas in with existing research you have found.**

    Information literacy skills—find information in a research article (6), add to key words for a search (2), revise idea map (3), avoid selection bias/cherry picking (6), avoid confirmation bias (4), evaluate sources (7 and 8).

- **And so on.......**

Appendix B: Citing and Using Sources

Avoiding Plagiarism and Cheating

In U.S. universities, you are not permitted to present the ideas of others as your own. This is called **plagiarism**. If you do this, you will face severe penalties, including being expelled from the university.

Note that paying someone to write your paper for you is cheating because it is not your work and you are presenting it as your own. You will face penalties if you do this as well.

You may not use something you found on the internet without citation. You also may not copy unpublished works such as the work of a friend or classmate. You may not even use part of a paper of your own that you wrote for a previous class without first getting permission from your professor.

Copyright

If you have created something that has a physical form, such as a literary work, painting, or recording, you automatically have the copyright (unless you have signed a contract granting copyright to someone else who paid you to create it). If you present a copyrighted work as your own, you are breaking the law and can be prosecuted. As with any outside source material, you must provide source information to give credit to the creator.

Creative Commons License

Many works are now being created that you do not need to pay to get access to. That is, these works are not behind a paywall (do not require you to pay a fee) as information in a database would be. Rather than having a copyright, these works are generally covered under a Creative Commons License. Be aware that there are different types creative commons licenses: some allow you to use the work commercially and others do not; some allow you to modify the work; some do not. However, **for all sources that you use**, you still must give appropriate credit to the creator(s) using citation.

If the license allows you to change the work, you must indicate if any changes were made. You also cannot restrict anyone else from using the information or limit its use.

How to Give Credit to Outside Sources

A variety of reference and citation styles are used to give credit for ideas. Each discipline has its preferences, and individual journals may also have their own style that an author must follow. Table B.1 lists the general usages. **You must** know which style is common in your field to join the conversation and be seen as a scholar.

To give credit to the authors whose ideas you have used in your writing, you do it in two places: within the text (citation) and at the end of the text (references/bibliography).

TABLE B.1
Common Citation Styles by Discipline

Discipline	Preferred Style
Humanities	MLA (Modern Language Association)
Social sciences	APA (American Psychological Association)
Journalism and History	Turabian/Chicago
Engineering	IEEE (Institute of Electronics and Electrical Engineers)
Medicine	AMA (American Medical Association)

Giving Credit within the Text

Citations reveal that a specific idea is from another source and they do it immediately. In addition to helping the writer avoid plagiarism, the value of citations is that they help readers find the original source in your reference list and then seek it out if they wish to.

Table B.2 provides examples of what a paraphrase and quotation will look like with respect to style conventions for those mentioned in Table B.1. Important aspects to pay attention to are: what information to include, where to include it, and how to use the punctuation. Note that most styles require a page number for a direct quote.

TABLE B.2
Various Reference Style Conventions for In-Text Citation

Reference Style	Example In-Text Citations
Author name in text	
APA	*Paraphrase*: **last name (year of publication) + paraphrase** Wheaton (2019) claims that recycling of paper has not become more economically feasible. **Paraphrase (last name, year)** There is some doubt as to whether recycling of paper has become more economically feasible (Wheaton, 2019). *Quote:* **(last name, year, p. #)** "Some researchers in the recent past have claimed that profits can be made from recycling, but our results put this into question" (Wheaton, 2019, p. 13).

MLA	***Paraphrase*:** **last name + paraphrase** Wheaton claims that recycling of paper has not become more economically feasible. **Paraphrase (last name p#)** There is some doubt as to whether recycling of paper has become more economically feasible (Wheaton 13). ***Quote:*** **(last name p#)** "Some researchers in the recent past have claimed that profits can be made from recycling, but our results put this into question" (Wheaton 13).

Footnotes

Turabian/ Chicago Style has two common styles	**Natural and Physical Sciences** **(last name year, p. #)** There is some doubt as to whether recycling of paper has become more economically feasible (Wheaton 2019, 13). "Some researchers in the recent past have claimed that profits can be made from recycling, but our results put this into question" (Wheaton, 2019, p. 13). **Humanities/Social Sciences** **superscript number** There is some doubt as to whether recycling of paper has become more economically feasible.[1] "Some researchers in the recent past have claimed that profits can be made from recycling, but our results put this into question."[1] - Notes are arranged in numerical order at the foot of the page (Footnotes) or at the end of the paper (Endnotes). - Notes should include the complete bibliographic information when cited the first time.

AMA	*Paraphrase*: Immunotherapy is a new class of cancer therapy that works with a patient's immune system to fight against the cells of a tumor.[1] As reported previously,[1]… *Quote:* "Immunotherapy is a new class of cancer therapy that works with a patient's immune system to fight against the cells of a tumor."[1]
Source assigned a number	
IEEE	*Paraphrase*: **[source number in order of which it appears in the paper]** Wheaton [1] questions whether recycling has become more economically feasible.
	Quote: "Some researchers in the recent past have claimed that profits can be made from recycling, but our results put this into question [1]."

Giving Credit at the End of the Text

Compiling a list of the sources at the end of your paper is called a **Reference list** or **Bibliography.** The publication information for each source is provided in this list so that readers can go to those sources if they want to read more or use this source for their own writing as well.

Therefore, citations and reference lists not only allow an author to give proper credit, but they also act as clues in the search for more information—they are another aspect of the research process.

As with citations, the content and format of a reference in the reference list depends on the style that you are using. Online sources such as university library sites and Purdue OWL have many examples of how to present different source types in a reference list using a variety of styles.

See *The ESL Writer's Handbook*, *2nd Edition* (Carlock, Eberhardt, Horst, & Menasche, 2018) or *The International Student's Guide to Writing a Research Paper* (Carlock, Eberhardt, Horst, & Kolenich, 2017) (both published by the University of Michigan Press) for a more in-depth explanation and examples of MLA and APA style conventions.

Other Ways to Create a Reference List or Bibliography

Another option that you have for creating citations for your reference list is using a bibliography creator like Easybib, Zotero, or Citation Machine.

Your university will subscribe to at least one citation manager programs, which allow you to manage the sources that you have found. Once you import your sources into the citation manager, it will find the publication information for you and then put it into the style that you require. Most important, you can import directly into the citation manager as you conduct your search so that you do not forget the key words that you used or lose valuable sources because you forgot to write them down.

Appendix C: Lesson Checklists

These checklists have been designed to be a useful a tool to help the teacher and the student evaluate the strengths and weaknesses of student information literacy skills displayed in the student's writing or in the lessons. The lists can be used to determine the quality of the work or as a reminder to reflect on the research process and on how skills are developing. This is also a good time to note any gaps or make improvements.

Checklist 1 (Lesson 1)

Scope of Research: Topic Choice

1. The topic fits the requirements of the assignment.
2. The scope of the topic matches assignment requirements.
3. The student's work with identifying information gaps and reflection on the topic demonstrate that the student has a clear idea of how to proceed with finding relevant research for this topic.

Comments and/or strategies for improvement:

Checklist 2 (Lessons 2 and 3)

Inquiry: Identification of Key Words and the Relationships between Them

1. The key words chosen from class materials show appropriate focus and are relevant for the chosen topic.
2. The key words chosen from related titles found in online search show appropriate focus and are relevant for the chosen topic.
3. The key words chosen from abstract and reference list of articles found in online search show appropriate focus and are relevant for the chosen topic.
4. The choice of key words and deriving of additional key words based on own thinking, as well as arrangement of ideas in idea map, demonstrate creative thinking and knowledge of how to determine and use key words.

Comments and/or strategies for improvement:

Checklist 3 (Lesson 4)

Confirmation Bias

1. Key words have been chosen to elicit a variety of viewpoints.
2. The list of titles found so far show that a variety of viewpoints is represented for a more comprehensive coverage of the topic.
3. The answers to Task 4.2 demonstrate a careful analysis of bias in terms of authors' language choices.

Comments and/or strategies for improvement:

Checklist 4 (Lesson 5)

Database Use

1. The databases chosen were the most useful for finding sources on the chosen topic.
2. The Boolean search strings created were useful for finding good sources for the chosen topic.
3. Boolean search tools and limiters were used in a variety of ways for optimum searching.

Comments and/or strategies for improvement:

Checklist 5 (Lesson 7)

Knowledge of Source Characteristics

1. Completion of tasks in Lesson 7 demonstrates student knowledge of primary vs. secondary sources, the information cycle, and source characteristics.

Comments and/or strategies for improvement:

Checklist 6 (Lesson 8)

Evaluation of a Source

- Analyses of audience and purpose show careful thought.
- Analysis of *where* carefully considers all aspects of authority.
- Analysis of *when* carefully considers all aspects of currency and place in the information cycle.
- Analysis of *who* carefully considers all aspects of authority (see p.80).
- Analysis of *what* carefully considers relevance.
- Analysis of *what* carefully considers accuracy.
- Analysis of *what* carefully considers comprehensiveness.
- The bias analysis for each characteristic is thorough and demonstrates a good understanding of how to recognize bias.

Comments and/or strategies for improvement:

Glossary

authoritative – used to describe information that is considered vaild because it was written by what readers consider to be an authority on the subject.

bias – when someone's perspectives or opinions influence information provided in a piece of writing

Boolean search – a search conducted in a database using the Boolean operators AND, NOT, or OR that enables the searcher to combine search terms to limit or expand the search, making it more selective or more broad, respectively.

citation – the information provided in a piece of writing that tells what outside source the information came from

citation manager – a type of software that one can use to format a reference for an outside source

confirmation bias – when someone selects information that only supports their opinion and ignores information that is contrary to their beliefs.

constructed – refers to the fact that authority of a source is determined by the values held by the reader and is therefore constructed by those values; authority, then, is not defined the same way in every context.

contextual – the context in which information is found help determine how to define its validity (see also *constructed*)

contextualize – when someone provides information to connect the ideas from an outside source to their own paper

creative commons license – a public copyright license sometimes available that allows a writer to use another author's work free of charge; usually one must still present a citation.

to credit a source – when a writer uses a citation to show that information came from another author

database – a place where one can find information that is structured in some way and can be searched

information gap – an area of the topic being studied that the researcher knows nothing about; making a list helps the writer see what he/she knows and does not know to further the research process

information literacy – the ability to find, identify, evaluate, and use information effectively, efficiently and ethically to investigate some topic or issue.

key word – a word or phrase that conveys an idea important to a research topic that is most likely used in many pieces of writing about the topic and that is used in a database search to find articles

limiter – something used in a database search to limit the type of sources found in some way, such as *year, journal type, language.*

open access –information/content that is available without a fee, usually through a library

paradigm – a theoretical framework or model

peer-reviewed – the process of ensuring that an article or book that has been examined by experts in the field and judged to be valid and valuable

perspective – someone's view on a topic

primary source – a first-hand account such as an interview (see also *secondary source*)

primary research – that conducted by the author of an article; the author's original work

reference list – a list of outside sources found at the end of a piece of writing that tells where the information cited can be found

relevance – the appropriateness of an outside source

scope – the breadth or narrowness of a topic to be studied

secondary source – a piece of writing that analyzes or explains an event some time after an event occurred

source bias – when a source presents only information that supports one side of an issue and neglects other information

validity – when the information found in a source is reliable, of good quality, and based on sound research

References

Bennett, E.M, Cramer, W., Begossi, A., Cundill, G., Díaz, D., Egoh, B. N… Woodward, G. (2015). Linking biodiversity, ecosystem services, and human well-being: three challenges for designing research for sustainability. *Current Opinion in Environmental Sustainability, 14*, 76–85. https://doi.org/10.1016/j.cosust.2015.03.007.

Bruce, C.S., Mohay, G., Smith, G., Stoodley, I., & Tweedale, R. (Eds.). (2006). *Transforming IT education: Promoting a culture of excellence.* Santa Rosa, California: Informing Science Press. (pp. 351–369).

Dogoriti, E., Pange, J., & Anderson, G.,S. (2014). The use of social networking and learning management systems in english language teaching in higher education. *Campus - Wide Information Systems, 31*(4), 254–263. Retrieved from https://search-proquest-com.authenticate.library.duq.edu/docview/1658674412?accountid=10610

Duncan, D. G., & Barczyk, C. C. (2015). The facebook effect in university classrooms: A study of attitudes and sense of community using an independent measures control group design. *American Journal of Management, 15*(3), 11–22. Retrieved from https://search-proquest-com.authenticate.library.duq.edu/docview/1726801047?accountid=10610

El Bialy, S., & Ayoub, A. R. (2017). The Trends of Use of Social Media by Medical Students. *Education in Medicine Journal, 9*(1), 59–58. https://doi-org.authenticate.library.duq.edu/10.21315/eimj2017.9.1.6

Ha, L., Joa, C. Y., Gabay, I., & Kim, K. (2018). Does college students' social media use affect school e-mail avoidance and campus involvement? *Internet Research, 28*(1), 213–231. doi:http://dx.doi.org.authenticate.library.duq.edu/10.1108/IntR-11-2016-0346

Haider, T. P., Völker, C., Kramm, J., Landfester, K., & Wurm, F. R. (2018). Plastics of the Future? The Impact of Biodegradable Polymers on the Environment and on Society. *Angewandte Chemie International Edition, 58*(1), 50–62. doi:10.1002/anie.201805766

McClure, K. (2017) Arbiters of effectiveness and efficiency: the frames and strategies of management consulting firms in US higher education reform, *Journal of Higher Education Policy and Management, 39*:5, 575–589, doi: 10.1080/1360080X.2017.1354753

Murray, D. (1975). Handguns, Gun Control Laws and Firearm Violence. *Social Problems, 23*(1), 81–93. doi:10.2307/799630

Perez-Carballo, J., & Blaszczynski, C. (2014). c. *Journal of Organizational Culture, Communications and Conflict, 18*(1), 29–40. Retrieved from https://search-proquest-com.authenticate.library.duq.edu/docview/1647822753?accountid=10610

da Rocha, R., Conradie, P., & Lombard, A. (2014). *Learner perceptions on the use of social networking services in education: A case study.* Kidmore End: Academic Conferences International Limited. Retrieved from https://search-proquest-com.authenticate.library.duq.edu/docview/1545530887?accountid=10610

Siegel, Michael,M.D., M.P.H., Ross, C. S., M.B.A., & King, Charles, III,J.D., PhD. (2013). The relationship between gun ownership and firearm homicide rates in the united states, 1981-2010. *American Journal of Public Health, 103*(11), 2098-2105. Retrieved from https://search-proquest-com.authenticate.library.duq.edu/docview/1448191039?accountid=10610

Also Available

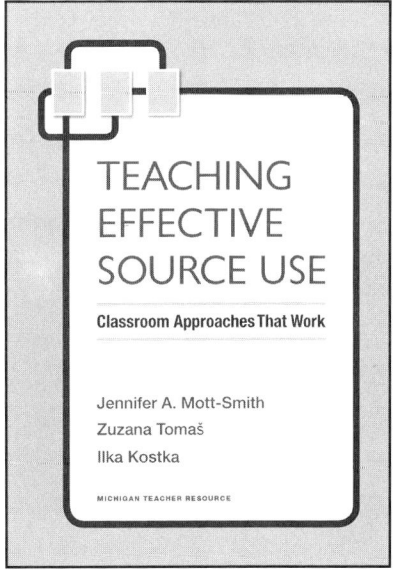

MICHIGAN

www.press.umich.edu/elt